The True *Revelation* of Jesus Christ

2nd Edition, Volume 1

DESMOND TEDDY

TO THE ONE WHO IS THIRSTY AND
SEEKS THE TRUTH TO DRINK
(JOHN 8:32; ISAIAH 55:1)

WESTBOW
PRESS®
A DIVISION OF THOMAS NELSON
& ZONDERVAN

WestBow Press books may be ordered through booksellers or by contacting:

WestBow Press
A Division of Thomas Nelson & Zondervan
1663 Liberty Drive
Bloomington, IN 47403
www.westbowpress.com
844-714-3454

ISBN: 978-1-6642-1124-7 (sc)
ISBN: 978-1-6642-1125-4 (hc)
ISBN: 978-1-6642-1123-0 (e)

Library of Congress Control Number: 2020921698

Print information available on the last page.

WestBow Press rev. date: 11/12/2020

DEDICATED TO JESUS CHRIST,
THE SAVIOR OF THE WORLD,
THE KING OF KINGS
AND LORD OF LORDS

Acknowledgement

I wish to express my sincere gratitude to the following friends and colleagues who helped me greatly to write the manuscript and did the proofreading and editing. Many thanks to young Samuel Nsowah who despite his tight schedule in his pharmacy education took most of his time to read and made good comments and corrections. I also thank Dr. E. Paintsil who has always been supportive and encouraging in this work. My sincere thanks to Lord Owusu Aboagye who despite his numerous assignments in his education in theology, got time to read through and gave advice. My heartfelt thanks to my wife Isi whose encouragement and motivation helped me through. God bless Sam, Dav and Alicia for spreading the good news about this book to their friends and associates. I also thank my dear friend and teacher Pastor Dr. Ferkah Ahenkorah who, apart from being a spiritual friend in this journey, took time to rectify the mistakes in the manuscript and not the least, Elder James B. who despite other challenges took the time to read the manuscript. On the rollcall of helpers are my own dear friend and brother Elder Emeka and my great in-law Elder Daniel, both for their constructive criticism that greatly improved the quality of this book. Lastly and most importantly, all the thanks go to the gracious Holy Spirit whose inspiration got me through this work to the end. I am grateful to every other person who have contributed to make this second edition come true but for one reason or the other are not mentioned. God bless you all.

Contents

1. Introduction

Writing a book about the Godhead and the person of Jesus Christ who makes the claim of God and man is not an easy task. The greatest investment in human history and in religion is to prove the credibility of a person who claims to bear the burden of the sins of the people upon Himself, yet He is rejected by men, even though it is written of Him that He is the Creator and Sustainer of the universe. To write a book about such a man, whose words have been used, misused and abused in the name of countless causes cannot be taken for granted. This is because we live in a world in which only prejudice and anti-Christian bigotry is tolerated. A world where hundreds of millions of people profess to believe and idolize Jesus, yet what He taught is seldom understood and followed. Almost no one grasped who He was, or what He did and why He was sent to the world. Not His followers, not His family, not the masses who listened to Him, not His friends and not even His enemies understood Him. Thus, to make a book of this nature available to the world entails challenges because of the diversity of opinion we find among people.

This is the second edition of my book *The True Revelation of Jesus Christ*. This is a further improvement of the first one, (*The True Revelation of Jesus Christ: To the Muslim, the Atheist, the Jew and a Light to the Christian World*), which I, as author, I believe will better serve the interest of readers. Besides, there are changes that are of considerable benefit in this edition that will enable the reader to enjoy the book. This work is therefore, divided into volumes 1 and 2. These new editions of two (2) volumes embrace the entire spectrum of human existence and prepare you with questions and substantive arguments to respond to your call as a citizen of the world and the Kingdom of God.

The True Revelation of Jesus Christ is hereby intended to serve as a source of inspiration to persons eager to know who Jesus Christ really is. Spiritual truths and matters concerning our world, coupled with the many religious paths each person threads, are of great interest to people with itching ears. This, among others, is what motivated me to write a book of this nature. Whilst the truth about Jesus remains a mystery to many, *The True Revelation of Jesus Christ* makes it easier to relate to Jesus in the most spiritual way. It sheds light on the person of Jesus Christ as the second person of the Godhead, the Son of God, and as the co-creator of the universe. Apart from such revelation, there are other sensitive issues regarding sin, redemption, salvation, and atonement that a person needs to know and understand. The reader is, therefore, made to understand that if members of other faiths lose their dogmatic approaches to religion, they would naturally embrace Jesus as Lord and Savior.

There is an exhaustive study of the literal and figurative implications of different Bible passages in this work. For example, when God makes the promise to Satan that He will "put enmity between you and the woman and between her seed and your seed", the book interprets this figuratively, pointing to the fact that out of this seed shall come one who shall destroy the evil that Satan brought. The only way to do this is on the cross, where there can be hope for an end to the misery, frustration, and pain that Satan brought to humans. It was on the cross that salvation was attained. The work of salvation, as stated in this book, is of greater importance, and the reader is encouraged to not take that for granted. It is best to take a critical view of the content and ask questions that demand careful consideration. How could a holy and righteous judge of all the earth give salvation to sinful people because of their good deeds if the Bible says all our righteous deeds are as filthy rags before God

(Isaiah 64: 6 NKJV)? Then it is clear that whilst Islam advocates for works as means of securing salvation, Christianity on the other hand through Jesus, says by grace the work is already done.

Conflicting approaches to issues of life are captured in the second chapter. The chapter investigates and delivers the true picture of the diverse religions and their surrounding contexts. It defends the gains of the Christian religion and its unique multicultural texture as a world religion. The book makes known vivid loopholes in the Quran and gives alternative suggestions as to what Muslims can do to critically examine these loopholes and address them with impartiality.

Further, the book reveals God's original plan, purpose, and foundation laid in a blueprint before the universe was conceived and was thereafter revealed. First, the master plan of God and His position as the supreme being of the universe. That it was the hierarchies of the Godhead with the attributes of will, wisdom, and activity, that designed, conceived, and worked the cosmic substance to produce our world. Among God's creation were perfect and sinless angels; one angel rebelled and brought about radical transformation in God's creation. The objective of this was to make our first parents sin – the result of which will bring endless glory to God. The overview of God's plan was, however, to make humans custodian over creation and that through humans, God could manifest in the flesh in order to salvage human from the chains of sin.

The chapter on the Godhead of the Bible, known as the Trinity, explains who God the Father is and who the Son and the Holy Spirit are. Examples and figures are hereby demonstrated to shed light on why and how the Godhead (Trinity) had its scriptural foundation in the Christian experience. The difference between God the Father and Jesus Christ is clearly explained for non-Christians and for certain sectors of the Christian faith. Whilst it is necessary to know the difference between God (Father) and Jesus Christ (Son), the common problem of Muslims and unbelievers about the so-called myth about the Holy Spirit being Prophet Mohammed is debunked in the chapter titled "The Holy Spirit." The role of the Holy Spirit as the most important being in the affairs of the earth is hereby fully underlined.

The central message in the book dwells on Jesus Christ as the ultimate source of creation. Jesus is seen in history as the most important personality with the convincing proofs that He once lived on earth and performed an assignment given to Him from above. The overwhelming weight of evidence placed on Jesus in this work as Lord and God of the universe is seen as unique and greater than any other testimony under the sun. The historical Jesus, unlike Mohammed, Krishna, Buddha and all the so-called prophets and great men of history, did not die and remain in His grave. Jesus is the only person that history can prove to still be alive today. History, therefore, debunked the fallacies of atheists and critics and gave proof by how the disciples of Jesus laid down their lives because of what they saw and witnessed with Jesus Christ.

The book further explains why Jesus being God is the first born of all creations. Thus, the controversial conception of the first born in human terms is explained in the spiritual sense to mean Jesus becoming the culmination and fulfillment of God's promise to bless all nations through the Prophet Abraham. The promise God made to Abraham, according to his faith and by his seed, to bless all nations of the world was directed to a single person - Jesus Christ. Jesus is put before all things because it is in Him that all things in the world are held together. Jesus, therefore, fulfills the intended role as God's firstborn son, who in His perfect life and sacrificial death was vindicated in glorious resurrection.

More to that is the mystery of Jesus being the Son of Man and the Son of God. The significance of this is Jesus's humanity; Jesus is fully man created like Adam from the dust but sinless in that He is fully God, which can be said of no other person. The reader is taken through this stage of revelation about the role of Jesus as our priest and mediator. By manifesting Himself in the flesh, He became like one of us to know our sufferings and have a Father-Son relationship with God.

The book further compares the evidence given in the Quran about Jesus with the Bible and explains why the reader should take the evidence from the Bible more seriously. The evidence about Jesus as both God and man and the Son of God is so strong that it makes more sense to believe in Him as such than believing Him to be just an ordinary prophet. Finally, Jesus in this work is revealed as the God of the universe. This is an important subject, especially for Muslims who want to understand what the Quran says about Jesus being God and the Savior of the world. The lordship of Jesus Christ is so important that the chapter on unveiling Jesus Christ is purposely to remove the scales from the readers' eyes and provide an open mind with food for thought so that *The True Revelation of Jesus Christ* and the love of God for humanity can be revealed.

This work is not in any way meant to condemn Islam or speak negatively of Muslims. I have many Muslim friends, and they are one of the best things that has ever happened to me. Most of them have understood the wisdom in this work and have taken the challenge to read the Bible from cover to cover, something their Imams seriously oppose. Out of God's own volition, humans have been given the freedom to choose. It is, therefore, imperative that people should have the freedom to make choices when it comes to what kind of religious faith they want to practice. At the same time, it is important that people have the freedom to learn whatever they want to learn in order to come to the full knowledge of the truth. Scripture says, "You shall know the truth and the truth shall make you free" (John 8:32 NKJV). Respect for the truth should inspire us to determine what distinguishes truth from falsehood and to help separate ourselves from dangerous fallacies.

2. Conflicting Approaches to the Issue of Religion

Many of the religious people in the world are of the opinion that all religions lead to the same God. The Moslems believe they worship the same God of the Jews and of the Christians. If all the religions are of one God, why the different doctrines and teachings, and why the religious conflicts? Why should Moslems, Jews and Christians differ in their approach to faith in God, especially in matters pertaining to salvation and redemption? Some people become offended when Christians preach that Jesus is the only way to God. The New Age movement advocates that *every road* leads to God and Christianity is one of them. If there are many ways to God, it will be the same as supporting belief in many gods which is polytheism.

For if there must be one true God, then there must be one true way to the true God and not many ways. The *true way* to God is not like travelling from London to New York. We take airlines and embark on natural ways to travel from London to New York, and we can do so from many directions. You may land in New York by airplane, by boat and even by car. It is not the same as going to God. That means, the way to God should be one true way that all believers travel. If we do not take the right way, many will miss the way, especially those who travel on the wrong tickets. That underlines the fact that the right way to travel is the key to arriving at your true destination. That is why there should be only One True Way. If there should be only one true way, then by which means can one reach the One True God? This one true way is Jesus Christ who points to Himself as *The Only True Way*. That means one needs to get the right ticket from Jesus possibly to embark on this true journey. That makes Jesus among all the various religious leaders of the world, the true and authentic way to God. For Jesus boldly affirms, "I am the way, the truth and the life. No one comes to the Father except through me" (John 14:6 NKJV). This means believing and obeying the God revealed only through Jesus Christ is the only possible way to get to heaven.

There must therefore be only one God, not the many gods of men. If there were many gods, there would be many ways to reach the heavens of the gods. Logically there is only one God and only one way to the true God. If there should be many gods, then these gods would not be infinite or supreme; therefore, they would not be God. The only truth therefore is that, since there can be only one true God, there can be only one true way to reach Him. For there exist many false gods and therefore from these many false gods, you arrive at many false ways which simply make these gods incompetent and unreliable. You may therefore miss your way to heaven if you must tread on the path of these false gods and their false ways with your soul.

If Christ then is the true way, then where stand the other religious people? Where stand the Buddhists, the Hindus, the Zoroastrians and the rest outside the box? Apart from reaching this one true way, do all these major existing religions (Judaism, Christianity, Islam, Buddhism, Hinduism, African Traditional Religion, Paganism, Mormonism, the Commonsense Family, etc.) worship the same God? Why should true worshippers of One True God make war against each other, promote religious conflicts, incite division, suicide bombings, malice, create separation and grievously suspect each other of evil manipulations? Why should countries like Saudi Arabia and Iran prevent Christians to live freely and talk freely about the Christian faith if we are dealing with the same God? Though the Christian identity in Western Europe is associated with higher levels of negative sentiment toward immigrants and religious minorities, it is not as dangerous as to practice one's faith. Why should Muslims kill Christians in the Muslim nations who refuse to deny their faith in Jesus Christ? Is it really true that all religions lead to the one true God and does it mean that there are many ways leading to God? Now concerning the non-religious people such as the secular person, the agnostic and the atheist, has the Bible not declared that a fool says in his heart, that there is no God? (Psalm 14:1 NKJV). If different ideologies and doctrines should create religious conflicts in the world, then perhaps not all religions are the same and people might therefore be worshipping or believing in different gods. However, if some religions hold in common certain attributes and ideologies from the same historical perspective, perhaps they might be worshipping the same God. That means religions supported and upheld credibly by historical affiliation may claim to worship the same God.

What about when the backings of history, ideologies and doctrines conflict with each other? How could Jews, Muslims and Christians serve the same God when they do not have a common ground on doctrines such as the Trinity or God having a Son or Mohammed being the last prophet? If Jesus traces His genealogy from Abraham, the father of the Jewish nation, where does Mohammed, the founder of Islam, trace his genealogy? If Jesus is the Savior of the world and the Son of God Most High, how could people assume that Mohammed, Krishna or Buddha can save them? Jesus and Mohammed are two important personalities whose followers claim to worship the same God. However, experiences of their followers about the knowledge of the One True God and mode of worship differ. Moslems claim inheritance from Abraham because of Ishmael, but what do Ishmael and Mohammed have in common with Jesus Christ? What about Judaism and Christianity? The Jews have the Torah, which constitutes a large portion of the Christian Bible and therefore provides a bridge between Christianity and the Jewish faith of Judaism. If there exists any common link between Jesus and Mohammed, there wouldn't be any problem between Moslems and

Christian. That would only have made it easier to trace their sources to the same One True God.

Whilst we consider the similarities and differences especially among the three major religions mentioned in this book, there is also the critical opinion of religious tradition that affects the pattern of thought, behavior and practice deeply rooted in people. The purpose of these religious practices to achieve the goals of salvation differ from each other. Moreover Muslims, Jews and Christians, have each a different understanding of salvation and God. The Bible, the Torah and the Quran have some similarities, however interpreted differently. This stems from the fact that they have different approaches to the truth. The critical observation made about some Muslims is that they have no time to study the Quran themselves. They only recite and do exactly what they have been instructed to do. The Jews on the other hand mostly have the written Torah passed on by word of mouth from generation to generation. In principle, religious indoctrination as seen in Islam is simply enforced and that makes some Muslims find it difficult to decipher the truth themselves about their faith and practice. This might be due to the result of strong tradition that binds Muslims together. In Islam, it is common to see people surrounded and supported in the faith by friends, families and neighbors. This indirectly affects their loyalty and so they become more committed, dedicated and easily indoctrinated. The fate of Islam and its culture is thus, interwoven. Islam binds Muslims together like a cord that cannot be broken. The positive side about this is that if all people could simply emulate such beautiful culture and affiliation, to stick together as Muslims do, the world would have been a beautiful place to live.

Although Muslims should receive praise for their unity and oneness in fellowship, there is not much freedom for Muslims to choose any other way than to remain Muslims for the rest of their lives. For a Muslim to leave the Islamic faith means often punishment by ostracism, death or other form of persecution. This is what makes Islam different from Christianity and Judaism; that owing to the use of coercion, individuals can find it difficult to convert to any other religion of their choice. When people are limited in their freedom to choose for themselves what they feel is right for them, it hurts. We find examples in the Arab Nations where Islam is dominant, and the right of individuals to convert to any religion of choice can be difficult. In this respect, the degree of freedom of choice in the Western civilization surpasses that of the Muslim World. The use of force by people in authority to suppress the right of others to choose freely in matters of belief is against fundamental human rights. The use of force by authorities, whether religious or governmental, creates chaotic environments. Similarly, the religious use of force to suppress the rights of individuals has promoted death and disaster in places like Syria, Iran and Afghanistan, all Muslim nations. The use of force is detrimental to human freedom and goes against the use of the gift of freewill which comes from God. If people believe that God is Almighty and that He is Omnipotent, they should allow God or Allah to work His own thing through the human heart. For Allah or God should be Almighty and capable enough to change the hearts and minds of people through the ritual practice of prayer as the faithful ones pray daily. The message of love, tolerance and forgiveness is of key importance to human freedom and peace. This is what the world actually needs.

Though force may be applied in certain religions, Christianity from its very inception has been a cross cultural and diverse religion with no single dominant expression. That is, regardless of a positive or negative attitude toward the surrounding culture, all Christians must respond to their surrounding context. It is from this that Christianity gains its unique multi-cultural texture as a world religion. Besides, whilst Muslims are limited in their choices, Christians on their own accord might reject a certain practice while others gladly accept it. This is the basic reason why the gift of salvation from God to humanity through Jesus Christ, should play a central role in the lives of Muslims and Jews and any other person on earth. The teachings inspired from the Bible and the Quran could therefore be the foundation for the differences in the two major religions.

To first mention the Bible, it is in its entirety inerrant. From cover to cover, one can see the tremendous, amazing, beautiful and divine work of God designed for man from the beginning of creation to the end of the world. Together, sixty-six (66) different books make the Bible, written in about 1500 years by forty (40) human authors through the inspiration of the Holy Spirit. The Bible was initially written in three languages; Hebrew, Greek and Aramaic. People from different background that wrote the Bible includes fishermen, priests, kings, physicians, and government officials. The Bible is an inspired word of God and Jesus is the center of every piece of divine work in it. Despite its authentic nature, many Muslims say the Bible is corrupted. The Bible is not corrupted as it is the inspired word of God. According to Webster's Dictionary, inspiration is "the supernatural influence of the Spirit of God on human mind, by which some prophets and apostles and sacred writers were qualified to set forth the Divine truth without any mixture of truth". That means it is the Spirit of God that led men to write the Bible. It also means every letter, word, sentence, punctuation in the *original text* was written under the influence of the Holy Spirit. Archeological evidences not necessarily named in this book and evidences and examples in this work provide answers to prove that the Bible is not corrupted. It is a divine book that speaks of matters of faith and morality and it is accurate with respect to science and history. The Bible is not exactly like the Quran. In the Quran, one finds in the various texts, problems of repetitions, contradictions and absurdities. How can an angel imparting a revelation to the author of the Quran do so with so many repetitions? Maybe Muslims may attribute this to lack of education on the part of the noble Prophet of Islam, but when it comes to spiritual things, ignorance and other limitations are not relevant, "For the Spirit of God searches all things, even the deep things of *God*" (1 Corinthians 2:10-16 NKJV). A person under the inspiration of the Holy Spirit or under divine impartation will not make striking mistakes with rampant repetitions, more especially when dealing with a book of this nature claimed to be the divine Word of God, though perceived as uneducated. With the differences found in both the Bible and the Quran, one will conclude that, there is no absolute strong connection between the two. Though there are many quotations in the Quran taken from the Bible, still there is doubt about the two coming from the same source.

Although Muslims categorically state that the Quran is a perfect book preserved on tablets in heaven (Surah 85:21-22), it actually harbors many contradictions. For example: "man was created out of nothing" (Surah 19:67) and "man is created from clay" (Surah 15:26). Since clay is something, there is a contradiction, which is, *"nothing"* and that excludes the possibility of *"clay."* Both cannot be true. Another examples is "You may divorce your wives twice: Keep them honorably or put them away with kindness" (Surah 2:229) and "Why, O Prophet! do you hold that to be forbidden which God has made lawful to you, from a desire to please your wives, since God is lenient, merciful?...Haply if he put you both away, his Lord will give him in exchange other wives better than you, Muslims, believers, devout, penitent, obedient, observant of fasting, both known of men and virgins" (Surah 66:1-5). This is in reference to the Bible where the Pharisees came to ask Jesus "if it is lawful for a man to divorce his wife?' "Testing Him... but from the beginning of the creation, God made them male and female. For this reason, a man shall leave his father and mother and be joined to his wife, and the two shall become one flesh; so then, they are no longer two, but one flesh. Therefore, what God has joined together, let not man separate" (Mark 10:2; 6-9 NKJV). There is a contradiction between what God intends in marriage from the point of view of both the Quran and the Bible.

From among the contradictions, there are instances of hate messages in the Quran against Christians and Jews that are quite disturbing. For example, in Hadith 452:177, the Quran tells Muslims "to find Jews, fight them and kill them" (Quran 9:29). This is contrary to the teachings of love proclaimed by the Bible and advocated by Jesus Christ that we should love our enemies (Mathew 5:44 NKJV). The Bible describes such attitude as the work of the enemy who is pictured as a thief here. The Bible says, "The thief does not come except to steal, and to kill, and to destroy. I have come that they may have life, and that they may have it more abundantly" (John 10:10 NKJV). Not humans finding their fellows to kill. Again, in the Quran it is written that Muslims should fight the people of the scripture, meaning the Christians and the Jews who do not acknowledge the *religion of truth* (which they term as Islamic religion) until they (Christians and Jews) are subdued (Quran 9:29). The Bible on the other hand, warns that all murderers and liars will end up in the lake of fire. (Revelation 21:8).

Whilst the Bible warns against aggression, hatred and murder, we witness the opposite in the Quran which proclaims that atrocities and aggression be exercised against none other than Christians and Jews. The reader should note that Muslims, Jews and Christians as well as all other ethnic and religious groups on earth are brothers and sisters and that is because they are of one blood (Acts 17:26-28 NKJV). This message of hate has unfortunately caused weak-minded indoctrinated Muslims (e.g. ISIS) to cast terror into the hearts of those who do not believe in the Quran (Quran 3:15) and *"cut off their heads and strike off every finger tips of them (Quran 8:12) and kill them wherever they are found"* (Quran 2:191). Unfortunately, Islam contradicts the core teachings of the Gospel of Jesus Christ, which is a message based on love. It is because of this love that God sent His Son to die the sacrificial and painful death on the cross. That is the overall message of the Gospel, together with the fact that we shall all be one in Christ and desist from hating or hurting one another.

Humans sincerely believe that striving for peace and unity is the most important thing the world needs. For that matter, we need to know why some Muslims sincerely believe that when they commit suicide and die together with those they call *"unbelievers"* by blowing themselves to death, they will gain the favor of God. There is no other way to explain this better than bringing this to the doorstep of indoctrination; that humans can unfortunately go to the extent of killing themselves because someone told them a lie. As humans, we owe ourselves the challenge and responsibility to truly look into all things and reject doctrines that do not promote common sense and good behavior. Humans have in general failed to question certain behaviors and why such norms of behavior be followed. Humans have forgotten that we first need sound principle, which should be our primary basis for taking decisions and for addressing fundamental truths serving as foundation for any system of belief or mode of reasoning. Whether religion or school of thought, principle will always look for basic truth or the source or origin of the truth. On what solid ground or evidence or by what justification do suicide bombers have to consciously blow themselves or commit suicide just to die together with *"unbelievers?"* Has anyone ever been to paradise and come back to testify of rewards for such extreme bloody actions? What moral reason is there for any good person with good conscience to strive for such a reward? What kind of a god is this that promises a reward of seven virgins in his Paradise if you only commit suicide and take others with you in your death? These questions bother the mind of many people. For there seems to be no logical answer to that. The Quran however, states: "I described to him how God would compensate the martyr sacrificing his life for his land. If you become a martyr, God will give you 70 virgins, 70 wives, and everlasting happiness." (Surah Waaqi'ah, 35–37). This kind of martyrdom, I think, is what Muslims refer to as Jihad.

We realize that this sexual enjoyment discriminates against women. For some women, as well as male unbelievers who die by blowing themselves up are not promised any sexual reward. In principle, it was because of the testimonies about Jesus that the martyrs of old were tortured and killed. During the earlier periods of the Christian church, through stoning, crucifixion, burning at the stake or other forms of torture and capital punishment, believers in Jesus Christ were murdered. None of them died voluntarily by killing or blowing themselves and dying with others to gain any reward in paradise.

Devoted and true Muslims need to examine this idea of Jihad critically to find the true intention of the writer of the Quran. Presumably the writer is advocating for a sacrifice one has to make for his land which is an earthily abode. A more probable motive is perhaps that the writer wrote this referring to the enemies of the

Prophet Muhammed during the time of the jihad, that it was equally good to sacrifice ones' life in a battle for one's country or land just to destroy the enemy, which did make sense. The Jihad had already been fought. In contrast, in the 21st century, there is no more need for Jihads in our modern world as the jihad has already been fought during the time of the Prophet Mohammed.

As we address the above issues with some seriousness, the same Quran addresses those who commit suicide (with the false pretext of venturing into paradise) with this warning: *"there is a devil attached to every person"* (Hadith 39:6757). This means the devil can make a person do a devilish act, i.e. commit suicide along with killing other people, believing that those who commit such acts will go to some paradise. The Hadith is hereby warning Muslims who commit suicide to refrain from such deception, since the devil can cause a person to commit such an act. There is nowhere in the Bible where a person possessed by the devil can do well or promote the welfare of others than to kill, to steal and to destroy (John 10:10; 1 Peter 5:8). In relation to the above observation, the Bible commands us "You shall not murder" (Exodus 20:13 NKJV). Christian, Jews and Muslims, like people of all other nations, are brothers and sisters of the same blood (Acts 17:26-28). Therefore, it is extremely wrong that some Muslims exercise jihad against any other persons the Quran terms as *"unbelievers"*. Once Muslims refer to Islam as a religion of peace, all Muslims irrespective of their background or where they live should be encouraged to demonstrate the spirit of peace at all times and should not be part of any suicide mission.

We are all brothers: Europeans, Africans, Asians, Whites, Blacks, Muslims, Hindus, Christians, all of us are from the same source (Acts 17:26-28 NKJV). God created all of us to love and to cherish each other. The earth and our universe belong to God and God loves all human beings equally. Though God loves us all equally, He also chose for Himself a people, and that is the Jewish people. God did so for the single reason that the world through the Jews will know the True God and that through the Jewish nation salvation will come to all. If the Jews are God's own chosen people, then Muslims who hate

15

Jews and want to destroy Israel need to advise themselves and think twice. God said to the Jewish people "For you are a holy people to the Lord your God, and the Lord your God has chosen you to be a people for Himself, a special treasure above all the peoples on the face of the earth (Deuteronomy 7:6, 14 NKJV). The Quran even confirms this in Quran 2:47 that "O Children of Israel, remember my favour that I have bestowed upon you and that I preferred you over the worlds". The Bible talks concerning Israel: For thus says the Lord of host: "He sent me after glory, to the nations which plunder you; for he who touches you touches the apple of His eye" (Zachariah 2:8 NKJV). Many Muslims have no idea of how intimate Israel is to God. Had they known it; they will re-consider certain actions the Muslim nations take against the nation of Israel. Take for instance the wars between the Arabs (Muslim nations) and Israel and more significantly the Six-Day War of June 1967, fought between Israel and its Arab neighbors that included Egypt, Jordan and Syria. In the six-day war, the nations of Iraq, Saudi Arabia, Kuwait and Algeria contributed troops and arms to the Arab forces with the purpose to defeat Israel. What happened? Israel won the war and significantly expanded its borders. We should not take the land of Israel for granted, for there is something spiritual and unique about Israel. Therefore, whether the atheist believes it or not, or whether Muslims want to fight Israel because of the Palestinians or not, it makes no difference; God will always stand by Israel and disgrace will come over any nation that makes any unholy attempt against the nation of Israel.

Whilst this conflict of war continues to remain between Muslims and the Jewish nation of Israel, one cannot put the blame on ordinary Muslims. The problem should come from the doorsteps of the Imams, who teach and interpret the Quran. The actual problems are the Imams and the Muslims leaders, together with their scholars planted in the various Muslim communities and Mosques. They have failed the people immensely and have manipulated the faith of the people only to suit their ulterior motives. Instead of teaching love that the Prophet of Islam should represent, some Muslims have suppressed the religion termed *the religion of peace* and in the eyes of the nations of the world, Muslims are seen in a negative light. None Muslim nations look at them with suspicion and that is due to ideologies taught by the Imams and teachers of the Quran. They have taught innocent people who could be of use and blessing to the world to commit suicide, with the notion that they will enter some paradise to enjoy sex. It is not the fault of the ordinary Muslim that some of the atrocities we witness take place. Rather, it is the Imams and teachers of the Quran who have taken captive the destiny of the Muslim world and have falsely indoctrinated the masses about Jesus. They have as a matter of fact, unaware of the scales in their own eyes, put heavier scales on the eyes of their own people.

Whereas some of us strongly oppose the actions of some Imams for their selfish ulterior motives and disagree with the interpretation of certain portions of the Quran; particularly with those aimed at certain groups of people termed as *"unbelievers"*; Muslims should also be recommended to read the Bible without fear. Jesus Christ the Lord and Savior of Muslims and Jews advocates the messages of love in the Bible and encourages all people, especially those who follow His teachings, to love their enemies and pray for those who persecute them (Mathew 5:44 NKJV). God wants a peaceful world and those who take the law into their hands to take the life of others according to the Bible, will receive judgement and destruction (Psalm 63:9 NKJV). It does not make sense if because of religion, a group of people send fear into the hearts of others only because they believe their religion is the only true religion. Surprisingly enough, everyone also believes his or hers religion is also the true one.

This refreshes my memory about a young man I met in the tram distributing tracts. He approached an elderly bearded man dressed in the Muslim traditional dress and handed over to him a tract. Upon doing so, he interjected: "Jesus the Son of God loves you". The elderly man retorted, "Jesus is not the Son of God, have you not read the Quran?" This sharp young man answered him, "Have you also not read the Bible"? Presumably, this was a sheer display of ignorance and lack of knowledge on the part of both. This is because neither of them has bothered to read the Bible or the Quran sufficiently enough to fish out the truth about who Jesus Christ really is. The man anyway rejected the offer to read the tract. The experience with this adult Muslim exemplifies how many Moslems simply fail to search for the truths in the Bible. On the other hand, many Christians have heard of hostile remarks from Muslims, and they have not taken the trouble to find out what the Quran actually says about Jesus.

Apart from the various contradictions stated in the Quran, there are other materials in the Quran originally taken from the Old Testament of the Christian Bible. This makes me recall my experience with my Muslim friends in Africa and in Europe who went to Christian schools. Most of them had no idea of who Jesus really was. This stems from the indoctrination they have gotten from home, that though Jesus was born of a virgin, He was only a Prophet of God. Dogmatism blinded their eyes and due to their faith in the Imams who taught them, they never bothered to read and find for themselves from both the Bible and the Quran the truth about Jesus Christ. It is however clear that Jesus appears many times in the Quran and in the Bible as the Creator of our world. However, Muslims blindly refuse to accept that this same Jesus is their Savior and God. Actually, dogmatism has led to creating a scene of display of religious superiority among Muslims who claim to have profound knowledge about Jesus over Christian apologists. Unfortunately, disputes and arguments among Muslims, Jews and Christians have mostly ended in tension and destruction of property. For each side claims superiority over the other, that their knowledge about the scriptures surpasses that of the other.

Eyewitnesses talk of debates at Parking Park in London where people throng during the day to listen to various kinds of religious arguments between Muslims and Christians vis-a-vis Jews. Other outstanding debates that have taken place between Islamic scholars and Christian apologists include Ahmed Hosen Deedat and John Gilchrist, and not the least Josh McDowell and Jimmy Swaggart. There was also Nabeel Qureshi, a former Muslim who became a Christian versus Miroslav Volf. Since Muslims deny the death and resurrection of Jesus Christ, most of these debates dwell mostly on sensitive topics on "whether Jesus rose from the dead or not and whether He is just an ordinary man like Adam or the Son of God".

The testimonies shared by some of these Christians who witnessed such debates prove that the Muslims in these debates have no basic ground to argue about Jesus, his gift of salvation and the work on the cross. They contend that Muslims have very limited knowledge about what Jesus did and stood for, and for that matter, they have to use the same critical eye they have for Christianity and the Bible in dealing with the Quran if they are serious about searching for the truth. Some Christians think the knowledge Muslims have about Jesus of the Bible is full of distortion and quite confusing to biblical truth. Others contend that the Bible was not to the Muslims but to the Jews, and for that matter Christians. Unfortunately, it is easier for Muslims to take the Bible out of context and explain it away differently from the way Christians do. This explains why Muslims would like to make Jesus look like a Prophet other than the Son of God.

Since the Jews and Muslims have rejected Jesus Christ as the Only True Son of God and the Redeemer of man, the challenge facing the Christian evangelists is how the barriers that are hindering the spreading of the gospel of the Lord Jesus Christ would be broken in the Muslim and Arab world. How would the Arab and the Muslim perceive and understand this great work of salvation? How do we go about to explain all the unanswered questions and mysteries surrounding Jesus and his birth? Would you say the journey of Christ to the world, His reason for coming and many other things that haunt our human imagination are just fairy tales or just mere fantasies? The atheists and the "Common Sense" families would not deny the fact that Napoleon Bonaparte ever lived and led France to war. That there were other great men like William Shakespeare, Abraham Lincoln, George Washington, Aristotle and even great villains like Adolf Hitler and Mussolini in history. If history records that these men lived, why do others fail to accept that Jesus ever lived?

There is also the odd fact that Muslims believe Jesus Christ was born of a virgin mother and did not die, and is still alive and will come back; yet they have more respect for prophet Mohammed, who was not born of a virgin and died and would not come back, than they have for the Lord Jesus. They claim Jesus was created like Adam, but was Adam not created directly from the soil and Jesus born of a virgin? The Jews on the other hand have refused Jesus as the Messiah and over 2000 years after his death and resurrection, they are still waiting for a deliverer and another Messiah. Unfortunately, for the Jews, no Messiah is coming again. There will never ever be any person born of a woman compared to Jesus who boldly and frankly identifies Himself with authority that He is the Christ, the Son of the living God. It is with this same authority that He affirms "He is the way, the truth and the life; and that no man can enter the Kingdom of God, except through Him". (John 14:6 NKJV). With this statement alone, all other religions and worshippers of other gods put themselves in serious trouble. For if Jesus is indeed is the way to God, it will be a total waste of time and a choice of faith with tragic eternal consequences to follow other gods or any other way. If Jesus further claims that He is the gate through which men can pass to find salvation; and that any other person who poses as the savior or the shepherd is a thief and a robber (John 10:1-9 NKJV), then it is high time we gave a second thought to the question of who Jesus truly is.

It is through understanding and discipline of one`s mind that the truth about spiritual things is revealed. The truth from this perspective is that Jesus is far different from Buddha, or Mohammed or Krishna and above all greater and superior. As independent human beings, we need wisdom as an important tool to make right choices and to give true judgment about all things. Making the choice between Mohammed and Jesus should be guided by principle and not by conviction of tradition or culture of man. That means principles should be the spectrum of the foundation and purpose by which every person lives the way they live. If Muslims reject Jesus as the Son of God but believe that He is coming back as Judge, it is because they have not understood God`s original plan, purpose and foundation for the world. Since Muslims believe that Jesus is coming back and the Quran tells those without understanding of the Scriptures first to ask Christians or Jews (Sura 10:94-95), Muslims should have used the scepticism they have about the Bible to test the validity of the Quran. For it is in doing so that the single purpose of God for sending Jesus to the world would be understood. In the light of this, we shall come to acknowledge that the truth concerning God`s original plan, purpose and foundation are all embedded and rooted in His Son Jesus Christ.

3. God's Original Plan, Purpose and Foundation

Before the foundation of time, God had laid down the blueprint of the universe. The blueprint was first laid in a Master Plan God had in mind before the start of creation and before man was brought into being. Thus, after God had created all things, He rounded up the end of His creation from the beginning. God stepped into Genesis to unfold the past into the present to include all creation. Unlike man, God always starts from the end. He looked at the conclusion and saw that it was very good. (Genesis 1:31NKJV). In considering the Master Plan, we take into account God the Supreme Being, who is also the Great Architect of the Universe. In the real sense He is God by name, but in actual sense the One God is actually a triune Godhead consisting of *the Father, the Son* and the *Holy Spirit*. God, characterized as *Boundless Being and* the architect of our world, is the source, the root and the goal of all existence in the physical worlds and the cosmic planes that emanates from the absolute. In the first chapter of Genesis the Godhead is called *Elohim* (Genesis 1:26 NKJV), which in the Hebrew is a plural noun. Elohim, then as threefold Divinity, have attributes that include *Will, Wisdom,* and *Activity.* Each of these attributes relates to each of the Persons in the Godhead. The Godhead worked together to create our world. As a result, the moment the First aspect of the Triune God was manifested as *Will* to create, it aroused the Second Aspect (which is Wisdom) to design a plan for the future universe. It was therefore the first manifestation of force in the form of imagination in the Godhead that conceived the idea of a universe. The Holy Spirit (which is Activity) working in cosmic substance, produced motion to cause time and space to move. This division of work and specialization was important to correct the *void, formless, empty* and the *darkness* that covered the earth that was separated from the depth of space (Genesis 1:2 NKJV).

Thousands of years earlier, this void and darkness of the earth had occurred due to rebellion of angels God created to minister to Him. They were created to submit to God in songs and worship. Among the host of angels was a perfect, sinless angel by name Lucifer. To say a little bit about him, he was created a supreme archangel. God placed a special light-beam in his countenance that shone around him and made him brighter and more beautiful than the other angels. Lucifer's name meaning the Light Bearer; he was made above every other angel in heaven, created in perfection, *a covering cherub*, and the one with the closest access to God and a guard to God's holiness (Ezekiel 10:1-14; Ezekiel 28:14 NKJV). In addition, Lucifer was a high and exalted angel, next in honor to God's dear Son, the Christ and had the honor to stand on the left side of God's throne. According to the Bible he walked *in the midst of the stones of fire* and occupied a place near to God just beneath the Glory, at the footstool of God (Ezekiel 1:27 NKJV). His appearance was beautiful and dazzling and he radiated light and glory. His beauty was flawless and breathtaking, and his wisdom was perfect. God made him so beautiful and covered him with gold and shimmering jewels. He then gave him the honor of a chief covering angel with a duty in the throne room of God. Talented in music, the Prophet Ezekiel describes his throat to be specially prepared to make him an outstanding musician. Some think he led the angelic choir. Would God decide to make an angel have such glamour if the angel was later to develop an evil nature just because of pride? The answers to these questions in this book are very important to consider.

Right at the dawn of time Lucifer was to bring about a radical change and transformation into the entire destiny of God's creation. Since he was involved in the government of God, it was relatively easy for him to take the step he took to plot against God. Despite God's good purpose for him, he was to turn God's perfect plan into imperfection and to prolong or delay the implementation of programs and duration of events designed by God and embedded in His Master Plan. As an anointed cherub, his heart was full of pride and that was because of his beauty. By the reason of his brightness, his beauty corrupted his wisdom (Ezekiel 28:13-15 NKJV). He exalted himself in his heart and was so entrenched in pride that God could no longer influence him. He was envious of Christ, and gradually assumed command, which devolved on Christ alone. Lucifer was able to influence a third of the angelic host to rebel against God. His intention was to unseat God demanding worship from the host of angels. The first outbreak of war in the universe therefore took place in the spiritual realm. The Son of God, who is the Prince of heaven and His royal angels led by Michael engaged in conflict with the rebel and those united with him. Lucifer and his angels were not able to prevail and were therefore, cast out of heaven. Lucifer's success rate was so astoundingly high that it seemed almost unbelievable how he could deceive and win the support of one-third of the angels and caused an insurrection in heaven (Revelation 12:3, 4, 7-9 NKJV). By far that was the greatest battle ever fought. After the battle, heaven was again peaceful and harmonious as it was before. Having been banished from the dwelling place of God, Lucifer now made the earth his abiding place with the sole aim of thwarting God's purpose. His first attempt to destroy things was in the Garden of Eden. After the expulsion, Lucifer's name was changed to Satan, which means the adversary and was also named the devil, which means the slanderer. The one-third part of the angels who joined him to fight got the names demons. Apart from the name Satan, he bears many other names such as Dragon, Serpent (it was in this form he used to deceive the woman), Beelzebub, Abaddon, Apollyon and many others. The prophet Ezekiel and Isaiah explain Lucifer's fall, and provide the insight into how evil entered God's creation (Ezekiel 28:15-18; Isaiah 14:12-14 NKJV).

Although Lucifer is the originator of sin into the world, God's major objective in His Master Plan was to fill the earth with His glory and that through His Son Jesus Christ, who is the Wisdom of God (1 Corinthians 1:24 NKJV), God's glory in the entire universe would be revealed (Psalm 72:19; Isaiah 60:1-3 NKJV). The Holy Spirit of God wrote this down in the hearts of the prophets to come, concerning His Son, that the world would know that by His Son all things were created: things in heaven and on earth, visible and invisible, whether thrones or powers or rules or authorities; all things were created by Him and for Him. God had declared from the beginning concerning His Son, that "He is before all things, and in Him all things consist" (Colossians 1:15-17 NKJV). God's Son was therefore to become the major focus of our world with the purpose to reveal God's nature as the Sovereign Lord of glory.

God had to reveal His nature to the world by His Son, but that was impossible without using the medium of the human flesh. He held a single purpose to create one man, and desired that out of that *One Man*, He would create a nation. His intention therefore was that this nation would be a guide to His creation and governance of man from the start. It is through this nation that the earth shall be filled with the knowledge of God's glory. God's intention consisted in creating someone in His own image who apart from taking the responsibility for His creation will eventually learn to develop God's character. On the other hand, God saw the end of His creation and realized that the nature of the man He would create would be corrupted. God could foresee that man, in the exercise of his gift of freewill, would make the wrong choice, and fall sway from grace into sin. Due to the fall everything made of dust of the earth was to manifest satanic glory, though God had a plan that this glory of the Arch-Enemy would finally come to an end.

Before God created man, He knew that man would need to go through certain experiences in order to become perfect. His dwelling place would be a place full of challenges and perfection would be a virtue worth striving for. In order that the man would overcome the challenges in life, power would be given to him to make choices, whether to strive for perfection or not. God saw the importance of experience to man, and so created all things in opposed pairs: male and female, good and evil, negative and positive. These opposed dimensions were placed before man to help him in the making of decisions and choices He was also given free will, which the man was eventually to use for his own benefit. This was intended for the man to control his destiny in decision making, either to obey God, choose his own way or surrender the glory God has given to him over to fallen angels.

The usual question atheists ask is "Why should God create the fallen angels if such a mess was going to be a disaster for God and man?" God could have stopped creating them to avoid them from rebelling but creating them was already in His Master Plan. In addition, that would have been far from the free will offered to operate and instead give birth to dictatorship. For Satan to be on the scene means man would have the license to exercise his free will in making choices and decisions making; for without the power to choose man would have had to function like a robot. Freedom to choose therefore was to be a cornerstone principle of God's government. Just as if God knew Lucifer would sin before creating him; He would have been repudiating the prime principle of free choice if He had refused to create him. Knowing well what Lucifer would do, God still created him anyway. What about God destroying Satan immediately after the insurrection? That would have led to fear. Some angels who did not fully understand God's character might start to worship Him through fear, saying: "*Lucifer might have been correct, be careful. If you differ with God, He may kill you.*" That would have settled nothing. Instead, this would have heightened the problem. This principle applied also to our first parents as well as every human being that appeared on the surface of the earth. It was the same principle God had counseled from the foundation of the universe that was to take place in the future (Ephesians 1:4-5, 1 Peter 1:19, Hebrew 9:26 NKJV). This simply means that God knew our ends from the beginnings. He knew before we were born how our lives would be lived, and even so, He permits us to live and allows us to choose between His government and Satan's. God knew for example that a person by name Adolf Hitler would be born to kill millions of Jews, but He allowed him to be born anyway. However, foreknowledge is not the same as divine predetermination. The principle of freewill also implies that, despite God's foreknowledge, Adolf Hilter still could have chosen not to do the evil he did. He had the free will but chose to do the opposite. God is therefore, willing to be misunderstood and falsely accused and be blamed for anything, while taking the time to allow every person to freely choose whom to follow, or what to do with their lives. This glorious yet crucial gift of freedom could come only from a just, open, loving God. It is an honor and joy to serve such a God. Thus, it became a principle by law that man would exercise his free will to guide his destiny.

God gave humans the laws of principles by free will, out of which God commanded all things to work together towards a common goal, which is perfection. His intention was to choose the weak things of the world to confound the things which are mighty (1Corinthians 1:27 NKJV) and declare His sovereignty at the end. In principle, God made laws that were to guide humans. These, meant to run in parallel with each other, were to allow negative and positive, good and bad, love and hate and-so-on-and-so-forth to function in the earth realm. God allowed that these be placed in the domain of worldly affairs to govern the areas of the sciences and the laws of nature and in the spiritual and physical worlds. Governments, institutions, nations, people, and everything under the sun and moon were placed under laws purposely to glorify God. Nature, including the sea, mountains and valleys, all had their purposes to exist only to glorify God (Psalm 148:7; Psalm 19:1; Psalm 96:11-12 NKJV). All would have failed had it not been that the Master Architect had shaped all things into course for perfect reasons, all to the glory of His name. God's main joy, however, was to be centered on man through His Son.

In the exercising of his free will in a world ruled by the evils of fallen angels, and with the power invested in him by God, man would learn to overcome and rule evil, though evil was to become a snare. Although free will was attached to man's destiny, God saw that man would choose to abuse such privilege by disobeying Him. The consequence of such disobedience would be the corruption of human nature and death, which was to be the penalty for sin. The result of this corrupted nature of man would be pains, sicknesses, diseases and catastrophes; however, nothing was to be left to chance. Everything in life would have to be embedded in God's glory and honor and likewise lead to victory for the man that overcomes. Man would never succeed in acquiring perfection, unless he focused on a single purpose, and that was to walk in God's commandments.

Despite the fact that man was made perfect by God (Genesis 1:31 NKJV), it was meant for him to undergo a test to prove his own perfection. It was out of this account that we see the first experience of Satan with humanity as given in Genesis chapter 3. Satan was determined to destroy man, the first important creation of God. Satan saw that the glory, which belonged to him from the beginning, was passed on to man. He was therefore cruelly determined to enslave and ultimately ruin man by sin. His major intention was to cause more sorrow, pain, and death than any individual or group in the history of the world. His intention was to take delight in destruction to make sure that persons, organisations and governments of the world are inflicted with pains and failures. He was also determined to make sure that institutions (e.g. marriage, families, churches) meant to declare God's glory are disgraced and that nations are brought down through wars and conflicts. His main agenda was to deceive individuals and families by the use of demons as agents of destruction. His first move therefore was to make the man God has created to sin. It is in the book of Genesis chapter 3 that we witness the account of Satan's first contact with humanity.

In Genesis is an overview of God's plan that included the creation of the first man and woman. In Genesis chapter two, God provides the details relating to creation. There were six creation days in the opening chapter of the book of Genesis pertaining to the preparation of our earth to sustain life. The earth already existed prior to the beginning of the days of creation according to Genesis chapter one verse two (Genesis 1:2). Before then God had unfolded His blueprint for humanity. What made the man unique was that he was created in God's image and made perfect and sinless to reflect the glory and nature of God. (Gen. 1:26, 27; Ps. 8:4, 5; Heb. 2:6, 7 NKJV). The intention of God for man was for the man to take dominion over all the lower forms of the earthly creations, including the entire universe (Gen. 1:28, Psalm. 8:4-8 NKJV) and over the animal kingdom. Before the fall, man could easily identify with God at all levels of communication, both physical and spiritual. He was able to communicate within his soul, body and spirit. These three parts of his being were in total agreement by the time of creation. Man's consciousness was initially directed inward, and he perceived spiritual things clearly as we perceive things in dreams by the time he was created. After the man had sinned, the three parts of his being: the soul, the spirit and the body lost touch with God. The oneness of his entire nature being dissolved, man now entered into conflict within himself and lost his spiritual perception. He failed to see from within and his brain became the link between his spirit and the outside world. That means the man could know nothing of the outside world except through the medium of the brain. In addition, he lost his spiritual touch and consciousness, the likeness of which was of God. That is the reason for the difference between the spiritual man and the carnal man. For the carnal man is dead to spiritual things (Romans 8:6 NKJV). Man is of the flesh and many people in the world today are dead spiritually and that is because they have not the spirit of God in them.

The book of Genesis mentions six times that the entire creation of God was in perfect shape before creation of man. The last time it says "…and indeed it was very good" (Genesis 1:31 NKJV). That means at the time of creation, the earth remained in a pure state without any human intervention. Death, decay, and all harmful things were unknown to the planet earth. The Bible records times when God would come down from heaven during the early hours of the evening and enjoy fellowship with Adam and Eve (Genesis 3:8 NKJV). God reveals man's divine destiny to inhabit the earth by commissioning our first parents to multiply and fill the earth. The Bible categorically confirms, "Then God blessed them, and God said to them, "Be fruitful and multiply; fill the earth and subdue it; have dominion over the fish of the sea, over the birds of the air, and over every living creature that moves on the earth" (Genesis 1:28 NKJV). As part of His plan for man, God commands man to take authority over the earth. He makes the earth the abiding home of man and a place prepared for humans to dwell. (Isa. 45:18 NKJV). His intention was that the earth becomes the eternal dwelling place of humans and that humans rules the earth, make it productive and beautiful place to live. (Ps. 8:4-8 NKJV). Though man was given authority over God's creation, God didn't state man was created to lord over others. God created humans equal, therefore it becomes wrong and sinful before God for man to rule and oppress man. In addition, God knew that the presence of sin on earth was to become a thorn in the flesh. He however provided assurance of His love, that no matter what happened between them, He will be man's God and His will shall always be done in man's life (Romans 8:39 NKJV). The Bible emphasizes on this, that "Your kingdom come. Your will be done on earth as it is in heaven" (Mathew 6:10 NKJV). This is because God wants the earth to have the same blessing that heaven enjoys. The original purpose of God therefore was to bring heaven to earth for man to enjoy a blissful life.

God's intention to make man custodian over His creation, was to share His goodness and grace of His majesty in abundance with man. There was nothing more pleasing to God than seeing man partaking fully in His glory. By virtue of this, God gave man divine moral guide on Mount Sinai, and wanted in return praise, honor and worship. Apart from the physical blessings, man was also to enjoy spiritual blessings with God. God gave man the power to become God's children. This was to give man the rightful access to heaven. That included the virtues and gifts of God's Holy Spirit and access to

God's supernatural gift in sharing God's nature which was to confer on man powers over every creature of God.

Although God created the earth to be man's eternal home, yet God forewarned man that his continued life on earth depended upon his obedience to His law. Before the man committed the first sin, God warned him to stay away from it. Here the power to choose between good and evil comes to display. As rewarding instrument, God gave the provision *obedience and disobedience* (Gen.2:15-17; Rom. 6:23 NKJV). God said to Adam, the first man on earth, that he would die if he ate of the fruit of the tree of knowledge of good and evil (Genesis 2:17 NKJV). Though he was not to die physically until after hundreds of years later, he was to die spiritually on the day that he sinned. This death termed as spiritual, meant total separation from God. The purpose of Satan's rebellion was to make Adam also rebel against God. Unfortunately, Adam and his wife fell prey to Satan and sinned against God. It was through the act of the first sin committed by man that God's divine plan for the world got contaminated. Satan claimed the possession of the earth (Luke 4:5-6 NKJV) and worked hard to manipulate the people on earth with lies (John 8:44 NKJV). Satan lured the man into sin and man obeyed Satan instead of God. When the man disobeyed God, the authority given to him over the earth realm slipped from him into the hands of Satan.

Had it not been that God had made provision in His Master Plan for man's rescue, it would have been chaotic and impossible to have obtained freedom and be saved. The death sentence pronounced on man would have separated him from God forever. Science says death is the cessation of communication with the environment, but when Adam sinned, not only was his environment affected; his sin separated him and every human being born after him from God (Romans 5:12, Psalm 51:5; Romans 3:23 NKJV). He not only lost fellowship with God; but also did the unthinkable by giving away his God-given dominion to God's archenemy. When such dominion was transferred, Satan took over man's heredity and handed to man death by heredity. The death condemnation that was transferred to his progeny brought sickness, death, and pain to the human family.

The Scripture says that "Death spread to all men, because all sinned" (Rom. 5:12 NKJV). A man dies because of his own sins, not because of his father's sins. That means every man is personally responsible to God. This is the reason why we see millions of people undergoing suffering and death. It was because of the sin of Adam that came sorrow, sickness, and pain and today many are experiencing mental and physical trauma, both young and old in every generation. This long period of human suffering is described in the Bible as a nighttime of weeping which has come upon the human race as a result of God's wrath upon humanity (Ps. 30:5 NKJV).

God's plan was for Adam and Eve to live forever with Him, but because of sin, immortality had to give way to mortality. Those who possess immortality live forever, but the life given to Adam and Eve was not necessarily immortality. If Adam and Eve had remained obedient to God and permitted to eat of the Tree of Life in Eden, they would have become immortal and therefore lived forever (Gen. 3:22-24 NKJV). Although immortality was part of the divine plan of God for Adam and Eve, they were created mortal. This means that not until they passed the test, death was a possibility, but not a necessity. Death for humans became a certainty because of sin (Gen. 2:17; Rom. 5:12 NKJV). When a person reaches immortality, he becomes indestructible. This is the same quality of the Divine nature of God that we witness about Jesus at the time of His resurrection (John 5:26; Heb. 1:3; Matt. 28:18 NKJV). Jesus Christ, by resurrection from the dead brought both life and immortality to light through the Gospel (II Tim. 1:10 NKJV) and the Gospel is the good tidings of salvation from death through the redeeming blood of Jesus. This means the Gospel of salvation was given to us in Christ before the world was ever created. God knew man would sin and therefore made provision for the gospel as a future option. The Gospel of salvation wrought through Jesus Christ is therefore God's eternal plan for man. This is the only plan of salvation whereby people may be acceptable to God to receive salvation. Though the Gospel of salvation was preached, men continued to relate to Satan and took delight to worship him and not to seek God. As a result, the wrath of God is revealed from heaven against all ungodliness and unrighteousness of men (Rom. 1:18 NKJV). By their own making, men have brought the judgment of God upon themselves. It was out of this that the Bible says God regrets creating man (Genesis 6:6). That is the same way people ignore, neglect and even push aside everything that relate to the truth and resort to carnal behavior, such as men sleeping with men, only to anger the righteous God of all creation (Leviticus 18:22-23; Romans 1:18-32; 1 Corinthians 6:9-11 NKJV). Men suppress the truth by their wickedness; know the truth but do what is evil. There will be no excuse for wrongdoing. Everything that reminds us of sickness and death and pain will be the result of our sinful nature. At specific times in the past when man displayed wickedness and rebelled against God, and divine forbearance was exhausted, there was no other measure for God to take than to destroy man either by flood or by fire (Genesis 6-8, 19 NKJV).

Since we have all transgressed the divine law of God through Adam's sin, we have been hindered to enjoy God's blessings to the fullest. This is because Satan reigns in the world and makes sure we remain blind to see and understand the glory of God in our lives. Adam's sin might have hindered us from receiving God's blessings for our lives, and though man transgressed the laws of God, it did not change the original plan. The scripture sums up God's will for us: "For the Lord God is a sun and shield; the Lord will give grace and glory; no good thing will He withhold from them that walk uprightly" (Psalm 84:11 NKJV). That means even in our sinful nature, God still has us in mind to save us. God is love and His plan for humans had been in the hidden even before the foundation of the earth (1 Corinthians 2:7 NKJV). Does God care so little about us as to allow death to alter the human destiny? Since we are humans, God sees our difficulties and at each difficult time in human history, and He has always been with us (Ps. 103:14). He did not leave Adam and Eve without assurance and hope, that at the appropriate time, the death sentenced placed upon them be lifted up. He told them, "the head of this same serpent who made them to sin would be bruised by the seed of the woman" (Gen. 3:15 NKJV). We cannot suppose that

Adam and Eve understood clearly the implications of God's statement concerning the seed of the woman. Adam and Eve had a sign of hope, for when their first son Cain was born, Eve said, "I have acquired a man from the Lord" (Gen. 4:1 NKJV). In the light of subsequent promises of God, it was now clear that God's statement concerning a seed that would bruise the serpent's head actually did mean that in God's due time Adam and his race would be delivered from Satan's rule, sin and death (Rev. 20:1-3; I Cor. 15:25, 26 NKJV). God's original purpose for creating man would be fulfilled and the earth would become one vast paradise, populated by the redeemed and restored offspring of Adam and Eve (Rev. 21:1-4 NKJV).

Since man could not save himself and the sin penalty demands payment beyond man's ability, how could salvation be achieved for man's total freedom? Since God saw that His blood would be the only remedy and requirement to pay the debt and set man free from the curse of death, He needed to come down Himself to take the form of man and possibly dwell among humans. It would have been impossible for God to take human flesh if He had not created man. The man was His brilliant idea, a feat to be achieved; and a great achievement human beings ought to be glad for: that God was to come down in the form of man to live among men. Man, made of the earth, corrupted in nature would need the one with the blueprint, to rescue him. God's final intention was to have many sons and daughters who would become perfect like His Son. His original plan, therefore, was to be fulfilled through victory over evil, out of which all the hidden glory in God's work would be revealed through His Son, the Christ. It was by this act of manifesting Himself to the world that God was to raise a nation for Himself.

To start a nation, God called the Jewish people by first calling Abram. It was His plan to bless all the nations of the earth through Abram (Gen. 12:3 NKJV). Later Abram's name was changed to Abraham, which means father of many nations. Abraham proved himself faithful by demonstrating his willingness to obey the Lord in the offering of his son Isaac. God then confirmed His promise to Abraham by an oath (Gen. 22:15-18 NKJV), that He will bless his seed. In the New Testament the seed promised to Abraham is identified as Jesus Christ (Gal. 3:8, 16 NKJV), the Son of God. He was the one to accomplish God's original purpose of blessing through the work of redemption. The plan of redemption that was established before the world began (2 Timothy 1:9-11 NKJV) literally means salvation and human redemption were planned before Adam sinned, just like the Gospel was given in Christ before the world was ever created. These were the only plan by which God intended to save the world. The Bible says "having made known to us the mystery of His will, according to His good pleasure which He purposed in Himself, that in the dispensation of the fullness of the times He might gather together in one all things in Christ, both which are in heaven and which are on earth - in Him." (Ephesians 1:9-10 NKJV). This is the truth that was locked up in the master plan of God for ages until God was ready to unlock the truth to man. The mystery is for God to gather and unify all things under the authority of Christ Jesus. That means there will the climax of history when the time given by God will come for complete fulfillment. This complete fulfillment of God's plan was to be executed through Jesus Christ.

God's plan was that Jesus was to come through the lineage of Abraham so that the whole world could partake in God's divine inheritance - hence Abraham received the honorific title *"the Father of Many Nations"*. Jesus therefore becomes the heir of Abraham not because He was Abraham's descendant, or a Jew with the advantages of a Jew, but because Abraham was full of faith and God was part of his life. This did not also verify the fact that Jesus was God because He was a Jew, but rather because He was also human. Though Jesus was of the seed of Abraham, He demonstrated what was universally human more than what was actually Jewish. This appeal was as the Son of Man and not as the Son of Israel or of Adam that Jesus responded to God and lived as both Man and God. In other words, it was not by any special Jewish rites that Jesus rested in God as His Father, but by what is universal and human and through obedience to the Father by prayer, filial love and submission. Jesus was to pass through these steps for our sake, that we too may be joint heirs in

His inheritance with God the Father (Romans 8:17 NKJV). The further explanation is that those who were to follow in the footsteps of Jesus Christ will be associated with Him as the promised seed (Gal. 3:27-29 NKJV). This means that true believers of Jesus Christ will participate with Him in the future work of blessing humanity with health and life.

Through Jesus Christ, the world was to experience the fullness of God's grace and glory in infinite abundance. Through Jesus, we were to receive God's grace free of charge. That is the reason why the scripture makes it clear that all things are in Christ, Christ is God's, and there is no good apart from Him. All that God did and laid down from the beginning was good in Jesus Christ. It was because of God's great love for humanity that through Jesus Christ, He made provision for Adam and Eve and their generations to be released from the penalty of death (John 3:16 NKJV). God's plan for the deliverance of humanity from death through Christ is corresponds to as well as reverses the condemnation of the entire human race through one man. We all lost life through Adam, and we all have an opportunity to regain life through Christ (I Cor. 15:21, 22 NKJV). This envelopes God's divine plan and many promises in the Bible assure us that when the divine plan for the deliverance of mankind from sin and death is complete, there will be no more sickness, pain, or death; that joy will replace sorrow, and that all tears will be wiped away (Isa. 25:8, 9 NKJV). This deliverance of humanity from sin and death will include the awakening of those who have died. These are those who would be *"redeemed"* by Jesus and afterwards be restored to eternal life (Isaiah 35:10 NKJV).

Jesus was therefore predestined to come to put an end to sin and death. The sin problem was to end just as it was in the beginning when everything was *very good* (Genesis 1:31 NKJV). As originally designed by the Creator, the Bible assures us that the human race will be restored to life. The plan of God is working towards completion, and the Bible reveals that now the time is near for the glorious consummation of that plan. Those filled with hope instead of fear are those who will understand God's plan for man. The good news is that Jesus Christ came to give us life in abundance! However, this abundance in God's blessed life does not come automatic. It comes by faith and obedience. The victory that overcomes the world is our faith. That is the more reason why the Bible says, "We have been made a spectacle to the world, both to angels and to men" (1 Corinthians 4:9 NKJV). Simply the entire universe would be witnessing as we each play a part in the controversy between Christ and Satan. As the controversy ends, every soul would fully understand the principles of both kingdoms and would have to choose to follow either Christ or Satan. Those who have chosen to ally with Satan would receive condemnation and those who have lived for God taken to the eternal safety of their heavenly home.

Through the Gospel of Jesus Christ, people from all nations and kindred will have eternal life, to fulfill the call of salvation, but only those who accept Jesus Christ as their Lord and personal Savior could be become the children of God's Kingdom. God's purpose therefore was to open the door to the Kingdom of heaven for all; both rich and poor, weak and strong and whosoever, and through Jesus Christ, calls upon men and women to simply believe and accept the offer of salvation by His Son on the cross (Rom. 2:7 NKJV). The faithful followers of Jesus Christ, at the time of the resurrection, would be highly exalted like Him (I John 3:1-3 NKJV), together with those called to be partakers of the Divine nature of God's promise as laid down from the beginning of time (II Pet. 1:4 NKJV).

God's final plan therefore in His blueprint, would be to unite all nations and people under Himself. That is the reason Jesus Christ would have to pave the way for the emancipation of humanity into one family (Genesis 22:18 NKJV). Apart from Christianity, which is the *True Spirit Religion of the Son*, there would be many religions. Under the various religions, families would be scattered. This would bring about discrimination, segregation, and even pain. All the religions apart from Christianity have been instituted by man out of ignorance purposely to further man's spiritual well-being under the lash of fear and the flesh. They have also been inspired by Satan to divert worship from the One True God. God's perfect plan is to gather all nations unto Himself through Christ Jesus and that would only happen through Christianity. For it is the Christian religion alone that would NOT be looking for the *One* who is to come, but for the *One* who is to come again. The purpose of the *One* to come again, God`s Son, would be to unite all human beings to consciously follow the law of love which is embedded in Christianity. No one would know the time of His coming, (Matthew 24:36 NKJV) however, we are commanded to preach the Good News of salvation. For until this reaches the uttermost part of the earth, it is likely that His coming might be delayed. By living this fellowship of love, which is the hallmark of the new dispensation for all nations, men and women across the globe have to accept Jesus Christ.

Jesus, the master designer of our world, together with the Father and the Holy Spirit shall fulfil the plan of salvation through the blood of the Son of God. This as mentioned above, is the blueprint of the Father. The blueprint that was laid down for the human destiny was so remarkable that, it serves great purpose of bringing to light this Supreme Being and to explain the complexities underlying His greatness, the One True God who also consists of three persons and is therefore known as *The Holy Trinity.*

4. The Tri-Unity: The Father, the Son, and the Holy Spirit

Having introduced the topic with God's original plan, let us get ourselves acquainted with this Supreme intelligent Being by name God. In this chapter, we will go into details to explain the difference between God the Father and Jesus Christ and to make known who the Holy Spirit is. What do we mean when we say God, who is He? The Godhead is the one referred to as the Trinity (Tri-unity), but the name *God* refers to a family of interdependent supernatural embodiments of the Divine Being. That is to say, *God* is the surname of that divine being. This divine being is like man but is not man. There is a Father in this divine being, who has a Son and operates by His Spirit. All the members of this divine being bears the title God because together they make up the embodiment of the divine being. Now, what if one drops out? Let us say the Spirit. In that case, there is no God. They need each other at every moment to operate as God. They are known as the *Trinity,* because they are three persons and operate in unison. In other word *tri* (i.e. 3)–*unity,* three persons bound together by their divine nature in an embodiment called *God.* They hate sin and therefore they are holy in nature, hence the name Holy Trinity.

To elaborate more on this; the word *Trinity* is figuratively used in the Bible and is a doctrine that is difficult to understand. This is how God is revealed in His Word about His Person. Anyone who believes in the Creator of the universe and in Jesus Christ understands the doctrine of the Trinity. The idea that God exists in three persons is not expressly taught in the Bible, even though it is there, hidden or implied (John 1:34; 14:16). This mystery of the Godhead could not be fully understood until Jesus Christ, the Second Person of the Trinity visited the earth. Jesus Christ however did not have to hide this concept an essential aspect of the salvation He came to preach was to make God known to man (Matthew 28:19; John 1:18 NKJV). The *Trinity* by definition is like a coded triangular wall where you cannot simply separate each from the other. Each wall of the triangle is a distinct individual entity in the Trinity. The diagram below may help us understand these individual members of the Triune God better.

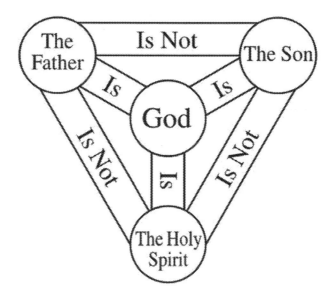

THE TRINITY

The diagram demonstrates what the Bible clearly speaks of God as God the Father, God the Son and God the Holy Spirit. It is as simple as calling One God: *Father is God, Son is God and Holy Spirit is God.* They are not the same, even though they are only One Supreme Being called *God.* You may not call this a reality, unless you get a more convincing proofs and examples. We can explain this further by doing some mathematics. Let us name it "*God the Trinity mathematics*". If you were to multiply God the Father - by God the Son - and by God the Holy Spirit, you end up getting one (1) as an answer. That answer *one* (1) is unique to God. If we were to use numbers, it will go like this: 1 x (Father) 1x (Son) x1 (Holy Spirit) =1. The same way when you add up the three together you end up getting: 1+1+1=3. This example is authentic and is universally accepted. That is because God is a *T-R-I-U-N-I-T-Y*, which makes God a triune God. Thus, the term: *Tri* meaning three, and *Unity* meaning one is Tri + Unity = *Trinity*. This implies that even though God is One God, He exists in three persons, which makes the three not three Gods, but One God in three persons. For example, when Jesus gave the Great Commission, He ordered His followers to baptize in the name (*singular*) of the Father, and of the Son, and of the Holy Spirit (Mathew 28:18-20 NKJV). If there were three different kinds of gods, Jesus would have said "*in the names of*". Instead, He said baptize them "*in the name of*". This means God in three Persons have different functions, yet they are one, co-equivalent, and co-existent. This is a way of acknowledging what the Bible reveals to us about God, that God is one, yet three *Persons* and have the same essence of Deity. Therefore, by definition the doctrine of the Trinity states that in the unity of the Godhead, there are three eternal and co-equal Persons (*Elohim*): Father, Son and the Holy Spirit and that they are the same in essence but distinct in role.

The account of the Trinity traces its origin from the beginning of time. The Bible lays account of the beginning of time and quotes "In the beginning God created the heavens and the earth" (Genesis 1:1 NKJV). In Genesis God spoke: "Let us make man in our image, according to our likeness; let them have dominion over the fish of the sea, over the birds of the air, and over the cattle, over all the earth, and over every creeping thing that creeps upon the earth" (Genesis 1:26 NKJV). Here God the Father was addressing the Godhead, which in Hebrew is *Elohim*. Elohim signifies a host of duel Beings. "Let us make man in our image, after our likeness" (Genesis 1:26). Note the plurality of Persons in the statement: "*let us make*", after which it consistently added, "He made them male and female" (Genesis 5:2). Here the translators have rendered the puzzling plural word *"Elohim"* as being the equivalent of the singular, sexless word *"God"*. When the Bible quotes God saying, "let us make man in our own image, after our likeness", *"Our likeness"* referring to the persons of the Godhead. The whole work of creation and grace is therefore, seen as a single operation common to all three Divine Persons in One, in which each person shows forth what is proper to Him in the Trinity, so that all things are *from the Father, through the Son* and *in the Holy Spirit.*

Man created in the *image of God* is likened to the Godhead. God created the man in His own image (spirit) and gave him a soul and a body. The *image of God* is the likeness to the real man, who is the Spirit man. The tripartite structure of man corresponds to that of the triune God of whom man is the image. The human spirit and body correspond to God the Father, God the Son and God the Holy Spirit. Just as the spirit, soul and body of the man play different roles, so do the Father, the Son and the Holy Spirit. The soul, the spirit and the body are not loosely connected parts of man. They are in unity to form one complete human nature. The soul is whole and entire in each part. It is like God, for it is partly a spirit with understanding and free will, and is destined to live forever, just like God lives forever. The man is a spiritual being and has a spiritual identity that is unseen even though he exists. He is identified as a spirit being for he emanates from God, who is a Spirit. The soul, the spirit and the body exist in one form, so also God the father, God the Son and God the Holy Spirit exist in One Eternal Form, thus *Elohim*. The soul, the body and the spirit are united and hence the word *"person"*.

When Jesus says: "I and my Father are One" (John 10:30 NKJV), it means Jesus claimed oneness with God in the sense of being equal to Him. We can get more examples to make this claim more vivid. For example, if you come to my house to look for me and you come by my surname, you will meet a whole member of my family bearing the same name. Using Andrews for example, if you come to ask for Andrews, which of the Andrews are you looking for in my family? Is it Andrews Thomas the senior or Margrethe Andrews our sister or Malik Andrews our last-born? So that if you come to the Andrew family looking for Margrethe, you need to specify that you want to meet Margrethe and not necessarily Andrew. When you call upon God, you call upon *Elohim*. Nevertheless, there are times you need the Father, the Son or the Holy Spirit and call them specifically by names. So that when you call my son by his name, he shows up personally by name. It is the same when you call upon Jesus by name. He is specifically different from the Father and the Holy Spirit and He hears you.

It is conceivable therefore that God takes one form but also have three different personalities. God knows that sceptics like the atheists and the Muslims might not believe the doctrine of the Trinity, therefore in His own wisdom He demonstrated this invisible divine reality by instances and concrete examples to make it easier to comprehend the nature of the Trinity. Let us use water as our first demonstration. Water is a good example of how one simple substance takes three different shapes or forms, and technically at the same time remains the same substance. Water can be liquid and can be solid (ice). It can also take the form of a gas (vapor/steam). You cannot see the process of water turning into a gas. You can only see the effect of gas after it rises to the top and lands on the surface. You can also use a cup of hot water and feel the warm steam rising to touch your hands. Even though there are three uniquely different states of water (liquid, solid, and gas), they are still water. We can therefore illustrate our findings in the measures as follows: The solid form of water, which is ice, reminds us of God the Father. Ice is hard as well as solid. In the same way, God the Father is our solid foundation. The Scripture says, "Righteousness and justice are the foundation of your throne; Mercy and truth go before your face" (Psalm 89:14 NKJV). God as a Person is solid and reliable and continues to reign in the world and in the affairs of men, bringing healing and blessings and compassion to all who call upon Him (Surah 40:60; Jeremiah 33:3). When we look at the liquid form of water, we think of Jesus who is God's Son. We use water to take bath or to wash ourselves clean. In the same way, God the Son died on the cross to cleanse us of our sin. The Scripture quotes: "How much more shall the blood of Christ, who through the eternal Spirit offered Himself without spot to God, cleanse your consciences from dead works to serve the living God?" *(*Hebrews 9:14 NKJV*)*. The gas form of water reminds us of God the Holy Spirit. Gases in the atmosphere (particularly oxygen, carbon dioxide and water vapour) absorb light, and have infrared wavelengths that we cannot see. The Holy Spirit also cannot be seen but His presence can be seen and felt in our lives as He works to make the will of God known to us, whilst He changes us to become more like Jesus Christ. Concerning the Holy Spirit, the Scripture quotes: "I still have many things to say to you, but you cannot bear them now. However, when He, the Spirit of truth, has come, He will guide you into all truth; for He will not speak on His own *authority,* but whatever He hears He will speak; and He will tell you things to come. He will glorify Me, for He will take of what is Mine and declare *it* to you. All things that the Father has are Mine. Therefore, I said that He will take of Mine and declare *it* to you". (John 16:12-15 NKJV). The scripture again declares concerning the Holy Spirit: "I will not leave you as orphans; I will come to you. In a little while, the world will see Me no more, but you will see Me. Because I live, you also will live". *(*John 14:18-19 NKJV*)*. The next time you drink a glass of water, use an ice cube, or feel the effects of steam, please let this lesson on water remind you that God is three Persons in One!

Apart from the examples above, an egg can be another beautiful illustration. Egg has a shell, and within the shell is the yolk and the albumen, altogether making a complete egg of itself – the shell, the yolk and the albumen. You do not call the yolk or the albumen or the shell alone egg. Each one of them forms part of the egg; the only difference is each part has its own name and function. This demonstration shows how the shell, yolk and the albumen of an egg is similar to the three persons of the Trinity. Apart from the different functions of the yolk, albumen and the shell, the whole egg goes through a period of incubation. At the end is the mystery of a live chicken, hatched out from the egg but only left behind the shell. Both the yolk and the albumen turn into chicken and not until the shell opens, it would have been difficult to see the manifestation of a live chicken. God is like the protective shell of an egg. In the protective shell of an egg is the yolk and the albumen. In God dwells the Holy Spirit and Christ. When God makes His will open to us, both the Holy Spirit and Jesus are manifest in our lives.

There is also another example the scientists call by name hermaphrodite, which in the study of biology is associated with the organism that has both female and male reproductive organs. This is an organism, which produces both sperm and ova at the same time. In the book of Genesis: "He created them male and female and blessed them. And he called them *"Adam"* when they were created (Genesis 5:2 NKJV). Here we see two persons bearing the name of one man called Adam, interpreted as *Mankind*. According to the Jewish teaching, the Man God created was a complete man but was made up of both sexes – *male and female*. Eventually God separated *the man* as single male and female and He called them Adam and Eve. This means God first created a man and inside the man was a woman (Genesis 5:2 NKJV). With the definition of hermaphroditic being, we know there was some time in human life when man had both sex organs (female and male) at the same time. In other words, until the separation of the sexes, the man was of both sexes (male and female). The Bible further explains that God put the man to sleep and out of his ribs, He created a woman.

From the scientific point of view the chromosomes can be used to explain this phenomenon. The study of Biology says the Female has two X chromosomes in her cells, (X representing female) and the male has both X and Y-chromosomes (Y representing the male). This means every male has both sexes - male and female in him. This is why a man's genes plays a more decisive role in his having sons or daughters and genetically speaking, each person has more DNA passed down from their father than from their mother. This explains clearly the nature of the man God created; that within (*inside*) the first man God made was also the woman. The idea of hermaphrodite Adam was therefore not the invention of the scientist, but of God. God wanted the female part of Adam to operate independently, therefore, He separated Eve from Adam, and even though they were separated, the Bible states categorically that the two shall be joined together and become one flesh (Genesis 2:24, Mark 10:8, Eph.5:31 NKJV).

Interestingly enough, unlike Adam, the chromosomes of Jesus, the Son of God was beyond human understanding, for it is rooted in the blood of *Elohim, the God of the universe*. The point therefore is this; if God initially created the man and inside him was the woman, and eventually He separated them as individuals (*male and female*) and put them together to be one flesh in marriage, it should not be difficult to accept or believe that God is three persons but is also *One God* (Trinity). This also defines the mystery in marriage, that the two shall be one (Genesis 2:24 NKJV) and what God has joined, let no man put asunder (Mark 10:9, Mathew 19:6 NKJV). What the scientist cannot fathom is how ordinary human sperms from a man injected into the ovary of a woman during intercourse produces a baby. Just consider all the complex structures: molecular and atomic structure, the bone structure and the blood vessels, the whole structure in its complex form with billions of cells producing a complete and complex human being. If this mystery of human anatomy and physiology is possible, then it should not be difficult for Jesus Christ *"The Word of God",* to be incarnated into human flesh, to live among people. Which one is easier: sperms and ovary becoming humans or God becoming a man?

The above analogies may be inadequate compared to what lies beyond our mortal minds, especially when talking about spiritual things. The belief in God as Tri-unity has not only its scriptural foundation but also its grounding in Christian experience. For whilst they were with Jesus, they gradually became convinced that the one God was *Father, Son, and Holy Spirit.* They knew already that there was the Creator Father; however, through examples and words of Jesus, a fuller understanding slowly emerged, that Jesus Christ is God and the Second Person of the Trinity. Eventually they came to realize more and more, that however human Jesus Christ was, He could not just be contained in human categories, but above all, He is God in human flesh. That was because Jesus did for them things that only God could do, even things that seemed to be impossible with man.

Therefore, for those who believe in God, the Trinity is not a speculative doctrine supported by scriptures; but beyond every experience God is one God *in three persons* and this is how Christians experience Him in *creation, redemption, and the new life that is yet to come.* In creation, God is the one that *thinks out* the universe before the beginning of any active manifestation including all the Solar Systems and the Cosmic. Jesus Christ, *the Word of God,* is the One who manifests everything that is in matter and combines into forms of various kinds all created things by the Spoken Word of God. Jesus is the Wisdom of God who spoke into being all things that exist in the universe. Jesus could not have done this until the Holy Spirit had moved (Genesis 1:2 NKJV). As mentioned earlier, *will, wisdom, and activity* are the attributes of the Holy Trinity. All of these pertain to the One True God. The activities of the One True God can be compared to a scientist undertaking an experiment. First, he has to have the *will* to begin with the activity. Then comes the *ingenuity or wisdom* to supply ways and means for demonstration. It is the same as *God having the will* and *Jesus Christ the wisdom,* and for *the Holy Spirit to carry the activity* of the Godhead in the universe. As explained in the previous chapter, God manifested as the *will* to create before the world was formed. Jesus Christ who the Bible says, "He is the Wisdom and Power of God" *(1 Corinthians 1:24 NKJV)* designed the plan for the universe. When the two *(God and Jesus Christ)* have conceived the idea of a universe, the Holy Spirit *(Activity),* the third being of the Trinity, made the move *(Motion)* to bring to pass the perfect will of *Elohim.* That is, He made an orderly motion to bring order when chaos was upon the earth. Jesus the "wisdom of God" had to guide motion *(Holy Spirit)* in an intelligent manner to produce definite results. So that when the Bible opens the sentence in the book of Genesis that in the beginning, God created the heavens and the earth, the Bible was speaking of the Hierarchies *Elohim* who is also One Spirit of God in manifestation. To throw more vivid light on this, the description of God is in pure functional terms. When God is creating the World, He is called Father. When He is convicting the World of sin, He is the Holy Spirit, and when He is saving the World on the cross, He is Jesus. This same mystery is incorporated into the belief and teachings of the Jews and the Muslims, but because they have ears but cannot hear and eyes but cannot see (Quran 7:179), (Mark 8:18; Psalm 115:6 NKJV) and above all cannot discern, the truth has been hidden from them. None of the human species on earth or plants could survive without the Trinity. When the scripture says: "in Him we live and have our being" (Acts 17:28 NKJV), it means none of us could exist outside the Trinity, for it is the Trinity that pervades and sustain our world with Their Life.

We find stronger evidence of this nature of God`s love in the Christian faith. The Bible declares that God is love, which means that love is part of God's very nature. (1 John 4:8, 16 NKJV). Love requires at least two persons. That means self-love is not really love at all. In Islam, such kind of love exhibited by the Christian God cannot be used to describe Allah, who according to the Quran is distanced from unbelievers (Quran 3:32). In Christianity, two persons in the Godhead are enough to demonstrate love. If God were only one person, then love could not be part of His nature. God demonstrates His love towards humanity by creating a family where the husband and wife love each other. The husband and wife demonstrate the same love towards their children. This is *collective love* existing in the Godhead and which appears in the family, the family as likened to the Trinity: *father, mother and children.* Therefore, those who believe in His Son (not under compulsion) shall not perish but have eternal life" (John 3:16 NKJV). To cap it all, God still demonstrated His love by giving us His Holy Spirit. The Father (God) and the Son (Jesus) will form our next topic. This is to enable Muslims, Jews and many others, get more clarification about the relationship between God and Jesus Christ.

5. The Difference between God the Father and Jesus Christf

God is the Creator and sustainer of the universe and the expression of all things. This Great Supreme Being who is the Source of our Existence, He is absolute and is beyond comprehension. Co-existent and co-equal with the Great Supreme Being is The Word, the Creative Fiat, *without whom was not anything made that was made* (Jn. 1:4). By Him was the flesh of all there is in the universe made, including the millions of the solar systems and the galaxies. This *Word* is the only Son, begotten of the Father before the creation of the worlds. These Three contain within themselves all things, they become more and more differentiated as they diffuse through the Universe. They are all present everywhere in the universe and are de facto *"near to all who call on him"*, (Psalm 145:18 NKJV). The existence of all things, therefore, has all the time depended on God and nothing in the universe could be sustained without these three persons of the Godhead.

Today scientists are stunned about the sophisticated coding within the DNA. More astonishing is the founding by molecular biologists, that the movement of creatures and their dependence upon one another have the various degrees of perfection found in them. Furthermore, there is the understanding that things come into existence and cease to exist, and that the marvelous order in the universe demands the existence of an *Almighty Powerful God* and the *Wisdom* of an all-eternal intelligent cause we call God. More interesting is the fact that, today scientists are speaking about God and from the revolutionary discoveries made from astronomy and molecular biology, there is the belief that the universe has a beginning and that the universe is just right for life and that the DNA coding reveals an intelligent Being, God. This is the work of the Holy Trinity. Even though the Father (*God*) and the Son (*Jesus/ Word)* differ in many ways, the Holy Spirit remains the Spirit of the Father and of the Son. The knowledge of the difference between the Father (*God*) and the Son (*Word/Jesus*) is so important that the reader is encouraged to pay attention.

Apostle Paul specifically explains this mystery of God and therefore says there is only one God and that is the Father. (1 Corinthians 8:6; Ephesians 4:6; 1 Timothy 2:5 NKJV). If that is so, why is Jesus Christ also God? There must be a reason as well as a difference. What Christians are saying is that the Father of our Lord Jesus Christ is the Father of all believers of Jesus Christ and there is no other God but that One God. Muslims and Jews have learnt from the chapter on Trinity how God and Jesus can owe the same title *God* yet are two different persons. The Jehovah's Witnesses (who wrongly deny the deity of Christ) and the United Pentecostals (also known as Apostolic or Jesus Only) affirm the deity of Christ but teach erroneously about the two separate personages of the Heavenly Father and the Lord Jesus. The Jehovah's Witnesses misrepresent Christians who believe in the Trinity by saying; *we teach Jesus is the Father*; while the United Pentecostals argue that *Jesus is the Father* meaning the Father and Son are the same person. These groups and their teachings have created doctrinal confusion. The Father and the Son both indicates plurality, and, in the Scriptures, the Father is distinguished from the Son. For example, Jesus mentioned, "If I had not done among them what no one else did, they would not be guilty of sin. But now they have seen these miracles, and yet they have hated both me and my Father" (John15:24 NKJV). The Jews saw the miracles Jesus did that confirmed that He came from God. Since they saw but rejected Jesus, they stand guilty of the most terrible sin; that is, rejecting God and

His Son. Jesus did many miracles that surpassed that of the prophets, and He did them by His own power and these should have been sufficient reasons for the Jews to accept Him as one sent from God, more than Elijah, or Elisha, but they refused Him. Jesus therefore told them that they have hated both Him and His Father (God); for they have rejected Him as the Messiah, despite the miracles and the doctrines He taught. Jesus in His dialogue with the Jews claimed to be the revelation of God, to be equal with Him. Therefore, to hate Jesus is to hate the Father also.

Although there is a difference between God the Father and Jesus, Jesus demonstrates His oneness with the Father by giving believers examples to follow. For instance, Jesus was talking to God that: "Now I am no longer in the world, but these are in the world, and I come to You. Holy Father keep through Your name those whom You have given Me, that they may be one as We are" (John 17:11 NKJV). Jesus was concerned about those who accepted Him and pleaded with the Father (God), that He would keep them by His power and for His glory and that, they might be united in affection just like the union between *the Father* and *the Son*. His prayer to God was that His disciples would escape the rage of men and be able to accomplish the great work for the glory of God, and for the benefit of humanity. Jesus emphasized on this oneness by saying: "And the glory which You gave Me I have given them, that they may be one just as We are one": (John 17:22 NKJV). This is the central theme of Jesus prayers. Since the standard for unity is oneness between the Father and the Son, Jesus was praying for the same kind of unity to exit among Christians. "*Between the Father and the Son*" refers to one in unity, not one in person and shows that Jesus is not the Father. Jesus prayed that all believers might be one under One Head by their union with Him and God, through the indwelling of the Holy Spirit. This is the only way to convince the world of the truth about Jesus and find fellowship with God and the saints of God and for the world to believe that God sent Jesus.

There is also the prayer of Jesus, which says: *That all of them may be one.* This stresses beyond doubt the absolute necessity that Christians live in unity. Jesus has not taken over the world completely and that is because millions of people are lost. In order for millions to be saved, Christians need to collaborate in joint effort to reach the world with the gospel. The problem rests on believers having love for each other and the unsaved world. Jesus thereby grants Christians the power to embrace the source of unity, which is the indwelling presence of Christ within the life of Christians. The emphasis of Jesus concerning love and unity was so important that all Christians ought to emulate it. Jesus further stated that "I in them and You in Me; that they may be made perfect in one, and that the world may know that You have sent Me, and have loved them as You have loved Me" (John 17:23 NKJV). This means Jesus Christ is in us, being the Omnipresent. He is able to communicate His divine person in every form. His blood to be shed will cover His people. His name would become assets to be inherited by the Saints. His righteousness will take possession of us communicating His grace and fellowship within the body of Christ. His prayer to God was that the Saints would be made perfect in knowledge and in holiness, in peace and in joy and love, and that by manifestation of the work of God in the lives of Christians, the world will witness the hand of God and believe in the Father and the Son. There is therefore a great burden upon Christians, and that is to love one another to be able to win the world for Jesus. The source of unity for a Christian is the indwelling presence of Jesus Christ by His Spirit. Christians have to remember that God is in Christ, and the presence of Christ in Christians means that God dwells in them. That makes Christians to actually partake of the divine nature of God (1 Peter 1:4 NKJV).

Jesus also uses judgement to explain the difference between Him and God. He therefore taught the following: "But if I do judge, my decisions are right, because I am not alone. I stand with the Father, who sent me. In your own law, it is written that the testimony of two men is valid. I am one who testifies for myself; my other witness is the Father (God), who sent me. Then they said to Him, "Where is Your Father?" Jesus answered, "You know neither Me nor My Father. If you had known Me, you would have known My Father also" (John 8:16–19 NKJV). Jesus was saying that He was not alone. He did not speak nor act alone. The Father (God) was with Him and the Father (God) sent Him; therefore, what He claimed and did was of the Father (God). There are separate and distinct personages on display when referring to Jesus and the Father. Jesus called God *Father* and referred to His mission: *The Father that sent me.* That means Jesus had a Father-Son relationship with God. God is His Father and He had come from the household of His Father in Heaven. Therefore, He alone could know all the facts concerning God (The Father). Jesus had come from God (The Father) to proclaim the glorious message of salvation to the world. Therefore, He said: "I am the light of the world. He who follows Me shall not walk in darkness but have the light of life" (John 8:12 NKJV).

Furthermore, Jesus prayed to the Father. This also shows He cannot be the Father. If He was, then it means He prayed to Himself, which is ridiculous. In this example, Jesus called out with a loud voice, "Father, into your hands I commit my spirit (Luke 23:46 NKJV)." When He had said this, He breathed His last. On the cross, He was saying to His Father the time they agreed upon in heaven, that He would suffer and die for His people, has come and will be over soon. That hour was a time of great trouble, distress and darkness and it was the time for prayer. He prayed that God will glorify Him by supporting in carrying Him through to conquer the enemies of His people, sin, Satan, the world and death and that He would obtain eternal redemption for them at His resurrection. It was the resurrection that was to bring the exact glory, for Jesus at this point is to bring glory to the Father (God) even as He Himself also obtains glory. The suffering and death of Jesus Christ on the cross was to bring glory to God by the Holy Spirit as Jesus obtain salvation for His people. The Scripture also accounts that after Jesus said this, He looked toward heaven and prayed: "Father, the hour has come. Glorify Your Son, that Your Son also may glorify You," (John 17:1 NKJV). Jesus looked towards heaven, the seat of the divine majesty, the throne of His Father and prayed. Again, the Gospel claims that

Jesus used the word *Abba* thereby claiming affection and relation to God.

If Jesus is the same person as the Father, then you are going to have to believe that Jesus sent Himself into this world. What about the one whom the Father set apart as His very own and sent into the world? Jesus asked the Jews, "do you say of Him whom the Father sanctified and sent into the world, 'You are blaspheming,' because I said, 'I am the Son of God'?" (John 10:36 NKJV)? In some Biblical quotation, it states, whom the Father *"sanctify"* which means to make holy; but this is not its meaning, as the Son of God was always holy. The correct word used in this version, is to set apart for a sacred use, to devote to a sacred purpose, or to consecrate to a holy office. This means God has consecrated or appointed His Son to be His Messenger or the Messiah to humanity. The Jews heard Jesus saying that He was equal with God. Jesus has many times applied this expression to Himself. He told them: *you charge me with blasphemy.* The word *charge* here is the use of the name of God that applies to Jesus. The truth is, Jesus did not deny that He meant to apply the term to Himself and He did not deny it was properly applied to Him either. Furthermore, He did not deny that it implied that He was God. He only affirmed that the Jews were inconsistent and that they did not have any authority to bring a charge of blasphemy against Him for using the name of God to Himself. Jesus distinguishes between Himself and God by saying "As you sent me into the world, I also have sent them into the world" (John 17:18 NKJV). Jesus states categorically how He falls within the divine will of His Father (*God*), what He was sent into the world to do, more especially to work out the salvation of His people. He is sending the same them into the *world;* first to the Jews and then the Gentiles and every part of the world to declare the mind and will of God.

The Father and Son must be understood as being two separate persons to make sense out of all of the aforementioned Scriptures. The Apostles Peter, John and Paul believed the Father and Son are two separate persons and wrote in that way. Similarly, ponder upon the following important Scripture, which like many others, proves

that salvation is conditional, as well as plurality between the Father and Son: "Who is a liar but he who denies that Jesus is the Christ? He is antichrist who denies the Father and the Son. Whoever denies the Son does not have the Father either; he who acknowledges the Son has the Father also. Therefore, let that abide in you, which you heard from the beginning. If what you heard from the beginning abides in you, you also will abide in the Son and in the Father. And this is the promise that He has promised us – eternal life" (1 John 2:22-25 NKJV). What Jesus said affects all human beings, including Muslims and Jews as well as atheist. It affects those who deny that He is the Christ, the Son of the living God. Anyone that denies that Jesus is the Christ, the very Son of God whom God had promised to send as the Savior of the world is the antichrist. There are two terrible things said about such person. First, the person is a liar and second the person denies God because of denying Jesus Christ as the Son of God. How does a person deny God if he denies Jesus Christ? If a person denies that God sent His Son into the world, then the person's image of god is entirely different from the God who is the Father of Jesus Christ. God sent His Son Jesus Christ into the world, so if we picture in our mind that God did not do so, then our image of god is not that of the true and living God. The true and living God has loved man perfectly and did the greatest sacrifice by sending His Son Jesus Christ into the world to save humanity by dying for man. This is when Jesus Christ took all the sins of man upon Himself by exchanging place with man so that man will live and not die but have eternal life. There is no greater love demonstrated by God than this. That perfectly explains that if any man says that God did not send Jesus Christ into the world, that He is not the Son of God, and did not die, then that person is thinking of some god other than the Father of the Lord Jesus Christ. If our Muslims brothers say Jesus did not die, then they need to give it a second thought and critically examine the words of Jesus carefully. It is only those who do not care about the truth and the salvation of their souls that will neglect such gift that leads to eternal life. In short, anyone who denies Jesus Christ

and says that He did not die for the salvation of the world denies the living and true God and is a false teacher and an antichrist.

Jesus continues to defend His position to the Jews by saying, "And the Father Himself, who sent Me, has testified of Me. You have neither heard His voice at any time, nor seen His form" (John 5:37 NKJV). No sane person would deny that people both saw and heard Jesus teach, but Jesus said the same people never heard the Father and never saw His form. We can only deduce Jesus cannot be the Father. God sent Jesus Christ into the world, so Jesus Christ naturally testified about God. The testimony included everything that God had ever revealed to man throughout the ages. Everything that God did in the past was to prepare the way for His Son, and prophecies and every move God made bore testimony that God sent His Son into the world (John 4:22 NKJV).

Other scriptures also show that Jesus could not be the Father: "But as I told you that you have seen Me and yet do not believe me" (John 6:36 NKJV). The Jews saw Jesus Christ, but they rejected Him. It is very clear that they were without excuse. The same applies to those who hear the gospel and fail to believe. They have every opportunity but rejected salvation and eternal life with God and have no excuse. When we address Jesus personally as an individual, there are other examples that show that Jesus was different from the Father. The Bible quotes Jesus as saying: "Thomas, because you have seen Me, you have believed. Blessed are those who have not seen and yet have believed." (John 20:29 NKJV). This shows the importance of faith in believing Jesus as the Savior of the world. That makes those who come to believe in Jesus without first seeing him demonstrate strength and warmth of heart. They are those who are sensitive to the voice of the Holy Spirit, accept Jesus Christ as Lord and God, and believe that He came to die for humanity.

There is also an instance where Philip, an Apostle of Jesus Christ demanded that Jesus shows them the Father. Jesus said to Philip, "Have I been with you so long, and yet you have not known Me, Philip? He who has seen Me has seen the Father; so how can you say, 'Show us the Father'?" (John 14:9 NKJV). Should we believe

Jesus is the Father? Many Imams and teachers from the Islamic faith explain this by saying that *Jesus did not mean He is God*. From the intellectual point of view, Jesus was not saying He is the person of the Father. He is not. Instead, He said that in Him we see how the Father would express Himself under the same circumstances. When someone sees Jesus, he sees a Person who has the very nature or the very character of God. He sees a person who has the very substance or perfection of God. Jesus Christ is not the same Person as God the Father, but He has the same perfect nature as God the Father. It is just like differentiating the yolk and the albumen from the shell and still have the substance called egg. You can take Jesus Christ to be either the yolk or the albumen and still take Him to be part of the egg, with the egg symbolizing the Trinity. If you see either the yolk or the albumen, you have seen the egg or part of it. Therefore, the person who has seen Jesus Christ has seen the Father in all the fullness of the nature of the Father.

Besides being an express image of the Father, Jesus rather is the outer shell in which the Trinity is contained when God is dealing with men. (Col. 1:9, 2:9; 2 Cor. 5:19; Jn 2:34; 14:10; Acts 10:38). What God in fact did was to turn the Word into human flesh. Then the Father Himself, being invisible, entered into the human mould of Christ whilst the Holy Spirit in His unlimited power and fullness rested upon Him. He who met Christ in the three years of ministry before His crucifixion and he who meets Him today was or is actually dealing with the Holy Trinity in one person: the incarnated word. The three are in principle separate but are united in Christ even though still separable. The difference between the Holy Trinity and the human trinity is that the three persons are both united but separable in the Godhead whilst in man the three persons (spirit, soul and body) are relatively inseparable except that the spirit alone can sometimes leave and return to the body e.g. during sleep, etc. I believe that the Father abandoned Christ at Calvary so that the Son alone could pay the full debt of sin for mankind in order to deserve the glory as Redeemer. (Ps. 22:1; Matt. 27:46)

The Scriptures go further to throw vivid light on this: "The Son is the radiance of God's glory and the exact representation of His being, sustaining all things by His powerful word. After He had provided purification for sins, He sat down at the right hand of the Majesty in heaven" (Hebrew 1:3 NIV). From the New King James Version (NKJV) it reads, "Who being the brightness of his glory, and the express image of his person, and upholding all things by the word of His power, when He had by Himself purged our sins, sat down on the right hand of the Majesty on high". The word in the KJV translates as *person,* which is correctly translated *nature.* There is also in other versions the following: "And He is the radiance of His glory and the exact representation of His nature and upholds all things by the word of His power. When He had made purification of sins, He sat down at the right hand of the Majesty on high". Still in other translation (RSV) it reads, "He reflects the glory of God and bears the very stamp of His nature, upholding the universe by His word of power. When He had made purification for sins, He sat down at the right hand of the Majesty on high". The word *exact* means the very mark or the very reproduction of God Himself and the word *representation* means substance. This means Jesus Christ is the very Being or the very Person and embodiment of God. That is the reason why Jesus Christ could be worshiped by the disciples (Mathew 14:33; 28:9 NKJV) and be worshipped by the angels (Heb. 1:6) and even prayed to (John 14:14, Acts 7:59, 60 NKJV), without committing the sin of idolatry, which would be the case otherwise as proclaimed by the Muslims that Christians worship man. This is only laudable because Jesus Christ is God (*by nature*). We have to bear in mind that what Jesus said belongs to God alone, which is worship (Mt. 4:10 NKJV). Therefore, it is not a surprise the angels are commanded by the Father to worship Jesus (Heb. 1:6)! Not to honor Jesus as the Father is honored is not to honor the Father at all (John 5:23). This is the first proof that Jesus Christ is the only Son of God and far better and superior to the angels. Jesus being the only perfect Son of God, was sent to secure perfection and righteousness for men. Jesus Christ is equal with God, because like the Father He is uncreated and self-existent and existed with the Father and the Spirit from all eternity.

Many contemporary Jews and Muslims find it wrong that Paul could distinguish *God* as the Father and the Son as *Lord* without any defense or approval. (From whom, I cannot tell). But the truth is, Paul treated these two divine names *God* and *Lord* as both identifying the one divine Creator and as a proper object of religious devotion but included Jesus in that divine identity. For Paul not stopping to explain or defend this idea simply reflects that the identity of Jesus Christ was not an issue of relevance between Paul and the Corinthians. He however wrote to the Ephes*ians* "There is one body and one Spirit, just as you were called in one hope of your calling; one Lord, one faith, one baptism; one God and Father of all, who is above all, and through all, and in you all" (Ephesians 4:4-6 NKJV). This implies that when a person puts his or her trust in Jesus Christ, God gives the person new birth and quickens him or her spiritually. (1 Peter 1:23; 1 John 5:1 NKJV). God also puts His divine nature into the person (2 Peter 1:4 NKJV) and gives the person His Holy Spirit which makes him or her the temple of God (John 14:16-17; 1 Cor. 3:16; 6:19-20 NKJV). God then puts the person into the body of people, His church also known as the body of Christ.

Paul emphasizes the Lordship of Jesus by saying that the Father cannot be Lord since the Son is said to be the one Lord. Obviously, this is not what Paul intended to convey, nor does he intend to deny that Jesus is also God when stating that the Father is the one God. In fact, by saying that Jesus is the one Lord, Paul is evoking the Old Testament texts also known as the Shema that is the Jewish creed of monotheism that say Yahweh is Israel's one Lord. In this instance, the Scripture quotes as saying: "Hear, O Israel! The LORD is our God, the LORD is one!" (Deuteronomy 6:4-9 NKJV). Paul's formulations are his way of expanding the Old Testament Shema to include Jesus within Yahweh's identity! Now looking at the Shema, which is the Jewish way of describing the uniqueness of God, the intention of Paul here is to include Jesus in the identity of the one Lord of the Jewish worshipping of one God. Paul has in fact reproduced all the words of the statement about YHWH in the Shema, "The LORD our God, the LORD, is one" (Deut. 6:4 NKJV), and Paul presented this in such a way as to produce an affirmation of both one God, the Father, and one Lord, Jesus Christ. It should therefore be quite clear that Paul is including the Lord Jesus Christ in the unique divine identity. The only possible way to understand Paul as maintaining monotheism is to understand him to be including Jesus in the unique identity of the one God affirmed in the Shema. This in any case is clear from the fact that the term *Lord,* applied here to Jesus as the *one Lord*, is taken from the Shema' itself. Paul is not adding to the one God of the Shema. That is to say, the Shema does not mention this Lord. Instead Paul identifies Jesus as the *Lord* whom the Shema' affirms to be One. Therefore, in trying to reformulate the Shema, Paul is saying that, the unique identity of God consists of one God who is the Father, and the one Lord, His Messiah, through whom all things are made.

From the forgoing explanations, we conclude that Jews and Muslims have not sufficiently understood the way in which the unique identity of God was understood in Judaism. It is certainly that Jesus is included in the unique identity and this makes Paul not to reject the Jewish monotheism of one God. Paul associates Jesus with the unique God, who is the only true God of Israel. That makes Paul`s placing of Jesus a clear statement taken from the Old Testament's doctrine that Israel's God is the one and only God, the creator of the world (Philippians 2:6–11 NKJV). This is critical, for it means that Jesus Christ is not like God the Father, but the fact is, He is God and that He did not just achieve a high level of righteousness on earth, but that He was the very embodiment of righteousness. This also means that Jesus Christ did not become God when He was on earth; rather He has been God throughout all eternity. Paul was led in his writing by the Holy Spirit, as he had all the time been under the inspiration of God's anointing. Therefore, in this revelation, he has kept the *One* intact with *God* referring to the *Father* and the *Lord* referring to *Jesus Christ* the *Son*. He does so by explaining that the identity of the *One God* also includes the *One Lord*. Paul uses the title

Lord in reference to Jesus by identifying *Christ* as *Yahweh*. In other words, Paul was not trying to say that Jesus is not God by calling him Lord, quite the opposite. Paul uses two divine titles, namely *God* and *Lord,* to affirm that both the Father and the Son are the one God, Yahweh. Further, Paul goes on to say "Therefore concerning the eating of things offered to idols, we know that an idol is nothing in the world, and that there is no other God but one. For even if there are so-called gods, whether in heaven or on earth (as there are many gods and many lords)" (1 Corinthians 8:4-5 NKJV). Paul refers to the gods and lords as the many gods erroneously thought to exist. Paul is classifying the pagan gods and lords under the same category of gods, e.g. the *many lords* of the pagans were not a class of inferior deities in relation to the pagan gods. In light of this, the expressions *God* and *Lord* are synonymous referring to the same category of divine existence. God and Lord do not refer to different categories of beings, but to the same level of Divine subsistence, to the one eternal Being of God. Finally, by saying that all things are from the Father and through the Son, Paul was again affirming the essential equality of the two divine Persons. Paul agreed with those who knew that *an idol* is nothing and are not gods, no matter what their worshippers may think. Paul says there is no other God but One God. He is the Father of the Lord Jesus Christ and all Christians. He concludes by saying there is one Lord, Jesus Christ, who is the only One Lord and Mediator who stands supreme between God and man.

Lastly, Paul gives more detailed and enterprising explanation concerning creation by stating that Jesus created all things for Himself: "For by Him all things were created that are in heaven and that are on earth, visible and invisible, whether thrones or dominions or principalities or powers. All things were created through Him and for Him. And He is before all things, and in Him all things consist. And He is the head of the body, the church, who is the beginning, the firstborn from the dead, that in all things He may have the preeminence" (Colossians 1:16-18 NKJV). This makes Jesus Christ alone the Sovereign Majesty of the universe. Everything in the universe owes their existence to Him. He holds the earth and space together, and He does so due to His love for us.

In conclusion, it is in Jesus Christ that God does manifest Himself personally and then shines His light on everything that is and is to come. Therefore, Jesus Christ and God are not the same person, but different personalities. This is a revelation that should be a blessing to Muslims, Jews, and many others with very limited knowledge concerning this subject. Furthermore, it is not enough to know only about Jesus and the Father without enough knowledge about the Holy Spirit who is the third person of the Trinity. This is why the next topic is especially intended as an enlightenment to the reader, as the Holy Spirit is the one at present directing the affairs of our world.

6. The Holy Spirit

In chapter 4 of this book, we talked about the Trinity and we have understood that the Trinity comprises Father, the Son and the Holy Spirit. We have also talked about the Father and the Son and have thrown light on their differences. In this chapter, we will deal with the third Person of the Godhead, who is the Holy Spirit. This chapter will help the reader to understand who the Holy Spirit is; the central role He plays in our lives and how important He is to us in the affairs of life in the shaping of our destiny on earth. It will also help clear away the misconception held about the Holy Spirit by some Muslim Imams and teachers. There are many errors in the Quran about what Christians believe and practice and one of the most significant errors lies in how the Quran misrepresents the Christian doctrine of the Trinity. That is because Mohammad mistakenly thought that Christians worshiped three gods, which he named as: The Father (God), The Mother (Mary), and The Son (Jesus), (Surah 5:73-75,116). Mohammed never understood the doctrine of the Trinity and that was because he never had any experience with any member of the Trinity nor understood their sovereignty. If he had done so, his message would have had no contradiction in relation to the message in the Bible. For the original writers (not translators) of the Bible were inspired by the Holy Spirit to write down the mind of God (2 Timothy 3:16-17 NKJV). That makes most of the statements said by Prophet Mohammed about Jesus and the Trinity false. If Muslims want to know who the Holy Spirit is, they can only be encouraged to read the Bible without partiality and ask for His guidance and they will understand the truth about Jesus and His Holy Spirit.

The belief of Moslems that the Virgin Mary was an aspect of the Trinity was a concept that occupied the mind of Mohammed (Sura 5:73-75,116). This was because Catholicism dominated the region where Prophet Mohammed lived. Catholics have great respect for Mary, the mother of Jesus, and it is certain Mohammed dealt directly with the Catholics and it might have been too late to make correction in the Quran by the time the Bible revealed that Mary was not part of the Trinity. From the entire Quran, there are many traditional distortions, which do not click well with the Bible. True Muslims are however, challenged to critically look into that. As the Quran itself advocates, if there are portions of the Quran Muslims don't understand, they should go and ask the people of the book (Sura 10:94). Muslims are therefore, instructed by the Quran to go to the Christians if they want to know who the Holy Spirit is. In addition, the Quran says that the Jews and Christians are members of the religious groups that abide by the Divine Books revealed by God, and they call them the *"People of the Book"* (Qur'an 3:64-71). These factors alone explain how serious we have to take the Holy Bible and its contents when it comes to dealing with the Holy Spirit of God. Looking at the concept and personalities of the Godhead in the Bible, Mohammed failed to understand the roles of the Father, the Son, and the Holy Spirit as important to God's plan of redemption for fallen humanity. That means in order to save us, God had to provide a sinless Man who could die in our place – the Son. In begetting the Son, and in relating to humanity, God is the Father. In addition, in working in our lives to transform and empower us, God is the Holy Spirit.

Many people have different views when it comes to the Holy Spirit. Some view the Holy Spirit as a mystical force. Others also understand Him as an impersonal power that God makes available to the followers of Christ. The work done by the Holy Spirit was seen the time the world was being created. The first biblical mention of the Spirit is in Genesis where the Bible says, "God created the heaven and the earth" (Genesis 1:1 NKJV). Focusing on a specific act of God in Genesis the Bible states: "And the Spirit of God was hovering over the face of the waters" (Genesis 1:2 NKJV). We see in the whole creation creativity that belongs to the Holy Spirit. The Holy Spirit is the one performing the spiritual activities of God in regenerating, indwelling, sanctifying, anointing and connecting with humanity as demonstrated in Acts 1:5-8 NKJV.

Being the third person in the Trinity, the Bible calls the Holy Spirit *the Spirit of the Lord* who is also Jehovah (Isaiah 40:13; Joel 2:28; Romans 8:9; I Thessalonians 4:8 NKJV). The Holy Spirit is as distinct from the Father as the human spirit is distinct from the soul. But even as the spirit of the prophets is subject to the prophets so is the Holy Spirit subject to the Father who is the decision-making center of the Holy Trinity. The Lord Jesus says that the Holy Spirit proceeds from the Father i.e. He is sent forth by the Father to perform His will. (Jn.15:26). The Bible compares a man and his spirit to God and His Spirit: "For what man knows the things of a man except the spirit of the man which is in him? Even so no one knows the things of God except the Spirit of God" (I Corinthians 2:11 NKJV). The former is not two persons, and neither is the latter. We speak of a man's spirit in order to refer to his thoughts, character, or nature, but we do not thereby mean that his spirit is a different person from him or is any less than the total personality. Nor does speaking of God and His Spirit introduce a personal distinction or plurality in Him. When we speak of the spirit of a man, we do not refer to another person but to the inward nature of the man himself. The man is his spirit and vice versa. The same is the Holy Spirit also called the Spirit of God. For example, Jesus said that in times of persecution God would give us proper words to say, "for it is not you who speak, but the Spirit of your Father who speaks in you" (Matthew 10:20 NKJV). Jesus spoke of God as our Father in terms of personal relationship, but with reference to supernatural indwelling and anointing Jesus spoke of God as the Holy Spirit. John 16:13 makes a conceptual (but not personal) distinction between God as Father, Lord, and Omniscient Mind and God in action, operation, or indwelling. The distinction is similar to that in Romans 8:26-27 and in I Corinthians 2:10-16 NKJV. The latter passage says we can know the mind of God by having the Spirit of God in us, for the Spirit of God knows the things of God. Nevertheless, as we have already seen, the passage clearly does not envisage a personal distinction in the Godhead, for it compares God and His Spirit to a man and his spirit. The Bible declares that there is *one God* (1 Tim 2:5 NKJV) and that there is also *one Spirit* and there is only *one body*, which is the Father, the Son and the Holy Spirit (Eph.4:4 NKJV).

In this world, we find different denominations and churches, but God is creating only *one body* of people who trust and follow Jesus Christ. In this one body which is also known as the body of Christ, God puts His Spirit into them so that they become the indwelling place of the Holy Spirit known as the Temple of the Living God. When the Holy Spirit dwells in the Christian who is a believer of Jesus Christ, that person bears fruit. This fruit includes love, joy, peace, longsuffering, kindness, goodness, faithfulness, gentleness, self-control. Against such, there is no law. (Galatians 5:22 NKJV). So that by the power of the Holy Spirit, God is creating into the body of Christ which is His church new people who are bearing the fruit of the spirit. These are those God wants to use to change people in our communities.

The Scripture emphasizes that we have one Lord (Eph.4:5 NKJV) and one God (Acts 4:24 NKJV). Interestingly, the Bible reveals that God is a Spirit (John 4:24 NKJV) and that the Lord is that Spirit (2 Cor. 3:17 NKJV), and that Lord is Jesus Christ (Acts 9:5 NKJV). The Lord Jesus Christ is identified as the Spirit: *"the Lord is the Spirit."* This does not mean that the Lord Jesus Christ and the Holy Spirit are the same Person. They are two different Persons, but they are one in their Godhead and Deity. This means that Jesus Christ is one with the Holy Spirit in the same way as He is one with God the Father. The three are one in mind, in spirit, in being, nature, and in essence. Therefore, they are one in will, purpose and work. The Bible again mentions that God was in Christ. For God to be in Christ also means the Holy Spirit was in Christ. We realize that God the Father, Jesus Christ and the Holy Spirit are all involved in the salvation of man. This is what it means when the Scripture says the Lord is that Spirit. It was the Lord Jesus Christ who actually secured our salvation and liberty, but the Holy Spirit who is actively involved in the revelation of the truth regarding salvation and the freedom from sin.

When the Bible speaks of the man Christ Jesus in relationship to God it uses the title of Father, but when it speaks of God's action in causing the baby Jesus to be conceived it uses the title of Holy Spirit so that there will be no mistake about the supernatural, spiritual nature of this work. We should also note that the titles *Holy Ghost* and *Holy Spirit* are interchangeable which should not confuse the reader; both are translations of the same Greek phrase. The King James Version uses the former more frequently, but it also uses the latter (See Luke 11:13; Ephesians 1:13; 4:30 NKJV). The latter is usually more understandable to modern English speakers, especially those unfamiliar with the Bible.

The coming of the Holy Spirit to replace Jesus on earth was a major breakthrough for Christians. Jesus was in the Upper Room with His disciples during the last hour of His earthly life. He at this point pointed out the most important subjects the disciples needed to understand before His death, revealing and filling them with the truth that was to take place after He had left them. They were to receive the very presence of God in the form of the Holy Spirit. Jesus therefore revealed to them the identity of the Holy Spirit. Jesus told them it was for their good and that of all believers that He was going to Heaven and that was because if He had not left the Holy Spirit would not have come. The ministry of Jesus Christ on earth therefore included the great promise to Christians, which is the promise of the Holy Spirit. The Bible reveals, "And being assembled together with them, He commanded them not to depart from Jerusalem, but to wait for the Promise of the Father, "which," He said, "you have heard from Me; for John truly baptized with water, but you shall be baptized with the Holy Spirit not many days from now". (Acts 1:4-5 NKJV*).

On the day of Pentecost, after Jesus had promised to send the Holy Spirit and left for heaven, the Holy Spirit came upon them. The Bible hereby quotes: "When the Day of Pentecost had fully come, they were all with one accord in one place. And suddenly there came a sound from heaven, as of a rushing mighty wind, and it filled the whole house where they were sitting. Then there appeared to them divided tongues, as of fire, and one sat upon each of them. And they were all filled with the Holy Spirit and began to speak with other tongues, as the Spirit gave them utterance". (Acts 2:1-4 NKJV). Jesus had to send the Holy Spirit because no man could live and witness for God with the arm of the flesh. Jesus knew that man needed a supernatural power, which is the presence of God Himself and the very power of God had to enter into the heart of man. Man will also need the very power of God in him to impart to him the divine nature of God (2 Peter 1:4 NKJV). It is through the divine power of God in man that man can be recreated completely (2 Corinthians 5:17; Ephesians 4:23-24 NKJV).

It was in the process of Jesus sharing how Christians are to receive the Holy Spirit in all His fullness and power on earth that Jesus told the disciples to *wait for the promise of the Father.* They are to wait in prayer for the coming of the Holy Spirit. They are to wait for the Holy Spirit who is the *supreme gift* of God to the world, particularly those who believe in His name and the work on the cross. The Holy Spirit needed to come to live within them, to give them the power to control their lives. They will need Him to proclaim the Gospel with courage to a world that would consider it foolishness, and often react in violence. The significance of the coming of the Holy Spirit and the importance of His presence in the lives of Christians make Christians better off than if Jesus were to remain with us here on earth as He was with the Apostles. This is because since Jesus left for Heaven, we have in the world today a *glorified* and *exalted* Lord of all seated at the right-hand side of God in majesty. Jesus is the Lord of all, and He rules and controls all in the universe and is able to fulfill all His promises to meet the desperate needs of the world through the Holy Spirit (Eph. 1:19-20 NKJV). That means that the departure of Jesus to Heaven made Jesus our Intercessor and gave us a Person who is able to sympathize with our weaknesses and to plead on our behalf right before the very throne of God. Therefore, it was good that Jesus went to Heaven and His place taken over by the Holy Spirit.

The Holy Spirit is the most important being in our world and in the lives of Christians. He is a divine person, a being with a mind, emotions, and has a will. Without Him, life on the planet would have been a disaster, more especially for the believers of Jesus Christ. He knows the thoughts in a man's spirit and that is because His presence is seen everywhere. "Where can I go from your Spirit? Where can I flee from your presence? If I go up to the heavens, you are there; if I make my bed in the depths, you are there" (Psalm 139:7-8 NKJV). Therefore, He knows the inner secrets of a man's heart. For example, when Ananias and Saphira came to the disciples and told a lie, the Holy Spirit already knew the intent of their hearts that they lied against the Holy Spirit. The Scriptures quoted that, Peter confronted Ananias as to why he had lied to the Holy Spirit. Peter said to Ananias "You have not lied to men but to God" (Acts 5:3-4 NKJV). Here the Bible affirms clearly that lying to the Holy Spirit is the same as lying to God. After lying to the Holy Spirit, the Bible says Ananias and wife fell down and died. In short, it is a serious offence to lie to the Holy Spirit. The Bibles says in this regard: "But God has revealed them [the good things God has in store for His children] to us through His Spirit. For the Spirit searches all things, yes, the deep things of God. For what man knows the things of a man except the spirit of the man which is in him? Even so, no one knows the things of God except the Spirit of God. Now we have received, not the spirit of the world, but the Spirit who is from God, that we might know the things that have been freely given to us by God." (1 Corinthians 2:10-13 NKJV). No one knows what is really going on in the thoughts of an individual except the man himself. But the Holy Spirit know what is going on in the thoughts of individuals. No one knows what is going on in the mind of God except the Spirit of God. Since the thoughts of God are unknown to man, the world does not know God nor the things of God. The thoughts of God must only be known by revelation. For the things of God cannot be seen, heard, or conceived by the mind of the natural man. The Spirit of God reveals them. Therefore, if we want to grow in maturity, we must rely upon the power of the Holy Spirit. As limited as we are as humans, we can never know the will of God or be able to do the will of God if the Holy Spirit does not come to our assistance. The Holy Spirit is a mighty God who knows all things and His duty is to instruct us with God's word and to lead us to the truth about God and the Lord Jesus Christ.

An important thing about the Holy Spirit is that He is the Spirit of Truth. One day Jesus met a Samaritan woman and said to her: "You worship what you do not know; we know what we worship, for salvation is of the Jews. But the hour is coming, and now is, when the true worshippers will worship the Father in spirit and in truth: for the Father seeketh such to worship him. God is Spirit: and those who worship Him must worship in spirit and truth (John 4:22-24, 14:16, 26, 15:26 NKJV). The Jews worship the God of Abraham, but their knowledge about the Holy Spirit is not like that of Christians. It is difficult for Muslims to understand how they can relate to the Holy Spirit as they have no testimony about the true worship in spirit and in truth. The belief in Jesus Christ and His Spirit by Muslims does not constitute the spiritual perception addressed by Jesus. In Islam it is believed that Allah is far away from those who worship him, and he has no child and that those who worship him are slaves (Quran 4:116). If God is a Father and His children worship Him in truth and in Spirit, then it will be difficult for Muslims to worship in truth as the Master they worship simply put fear in the worshippers. To worship God in Spirit and in truth means to worship God with the spiritual drive and ability of one's soul. It is in this kind of worship that the Christian seeks the most intimate closeness, fellowship and intimacy with God. Note that Jesus brought a change in worship. Jesus said, *"The hour is coming, and now is."* Before Jesus Christ, we have all the time worshipped God in special places like the temple in Jerusalem. Jesus Christ came to open the door into the presence of God so that one can worship God anywhere. This is because the Holy Spirit is God and is omnipresent and Christians can tap His source and presence from everywhere.

The wisdom of God is given to us through the Holy Spirit so that Christians might know the things that are freely given to us by God. This truth from the Holy Spirit is meant to change our lives and to reveal to us the secrets and hidden treasures of God. Through the wisdom of God by the Holy Spirit, we receive guidance to help us set others free from the troubles of this world. The believers of Jesus Christ who set their minds on spiritual things can understand the hidden and deep things of God, as they tune in with the Spirit of God. Just as the Holy Spirit reveals the Wisdom of God, He is also a divine person with a mind (Romans 8:27 NKJV) and because He possesses a mind, He can teach people. When a believer of Jesus Christ receives the baptism of the Holy Spirit by the laying on of hands, he is delivered from the works of the flesh. He begins to bear the first fruit of the Holy Spirit which we have already named (Gal. 5:22 NKJV). When a Christians is possessed the Holy Spirit, he bears fruit of the Spirit. That person begins to live abundantly and eternally by experiencing the fullness of the Holy Spirit. So that the life the person lives, coupled with the love he shows others and the atmosphere of peace and joy he enjoys, will cause others to come closer to God.

The Holy Spirit thinks only of good things (Acts 15:28 NKJV). That is because He knows and performs the activity of searching all things and knows the thoughts of God even the deep things of God (1 Corinthians 2:10- 11 NKJV). As a person, the Holy Spirit has feelings and He can be grieved. If the Holy Spirit can be grieved, then it means He has emotions (Ephesians 4:30 NKJV) and can be insulted (Hebrews 10:29 NKJV); but to insult or for that matter to sin against the Holy Spirit is very serious. Jesus mentioned that all sins would be forgiven but not the sin against the Holy Spirit, either in this age or in the age to come (Mathew 12:32, Mark 3:22-30 NKJV).

The unforgiveable sin against the Holy Spirit is willfully

blaspheming the Holy Spirit by calling Him a demon. Some of the Jews of Jesus' day did by attributing the miracles and deliverances of Christ to Beelzebub. God would not forgive them because they knew in their hearts that Christ was from God but chose to call the Spirit upon him a demon. They did so out of envy and to prevent the multitude from recognizing him as the Messiah. I believe this is not a sin many believers may commit in our day. A true believer cannot call the Holy Spirit a demon without denying Christ at the same time. If unbelievers, however, call the Holy Spirit a demon, the sin will be forgiven them when they come to believe in Christ since they acted in ignorance. It is clear therefore that the only unforgivable sin is permanently rejecting Jesus Christ as Lord and Savior (John 3:18, 3:36 NKJV). That means speaking against the Holy Spirit is the same as rejecting Christ Jesus Christ as your savior and Lord. For those who sincerely blaspheme the Holy Spirit also reject the Lord Jesus Christ at the same time. The principal work of the Holy Spirit is to convict men to accept the Lord Jesus as their Lord and Savior so that men will enjoy the Good News about the Lord Jesus; that the Lord Jesus came to save us from our sins and to reunite us to God (Acts 7:51, John 16:8, 1 Cor. 2:12-14 NKJV). If a person refuses to submit to the counsel of the Holy Spirit by calling what is good evil, then that becomes a serious offence against the Holy Spirit. Salvation through the blood of Jesus Christ is the grace of God extended to all humanity and to refuse such offer will automatically separate a person from God forever. That also calls for the fact that anyone who rejects the convicting work of the Holy Spirit and does not repent will not be forgiven, not in this world and neither in the world to come (Mathew 12:32 NKJV).

The Holy Spirit guides us by convicting us of sin (John 16:8 NKJV). This is really a good thing. The reason is that God wants us to get rid of the things that displease Him, and the only way to identify those things is when His Spirit convicts us. The Spirit works through our conscience to make us aware of sins in our lives. He helps us to stop sinning and to start doing the things that please God. The Holy Spirit delivers and saves a person. This is when a person has accepted Jesus Christ as his or her Lord and personal savior. As Christians face sufferings and persecution in this world, they have the greatest source of help that is imaginable, and that is prayer. Christians can approach God whenever needed and pray to God for strength to walk through to conquer the sufferings of the world and to receive forgiveness of sin. In most cases since we do not know how to pray, the Holy Spirit intercedes (*prays*) for the saints with groaning that is too deep for words (Romans 8:26-27 NKJV) and makes decisions according to His will (1 Corinthians 12:7-11 NKJV).

Sometimes due to the struggling and suffering, life becomes so heavy that we are unable to bear many situations and the Spirit leads us to pray with groaning that cannot be expressed in words. At other times, matters of great importance grip our hearts to such an extent that words cannot express our feelings. Emotions become too much for words and we become lost and speechless in the presence of God. We then go to God and say, *"Lord, I'm just not sure how to pray or what to say"*; the Holy Spirit helps us in those times, and actually intercedes for us, helping us to say the right prayers for us. Whilst we accept the fact that we are human and weak, it is the work of the Holy Spirit to help us in our weaknesses. If we are sincere and wrestling to pray, the Holy Spirit then helps us to overcome and control the emotional changes, takes control of our emotions, directs, and guides us. He helps us to control our sinful inclinations, quiets and stirs our hearts to draw us closer to God in every situation.

Another important fact to note about the Holy Spirit is His will to choose to give gifts (1 Corinthians 12:11 NKJV) and direct activities of Christians (Acts 16:6-11 NKJV). God's spiritual gifts do not come from any other source than the Holy Spirit. It is not possible for men to earn, merit or work to gain true spiritual gifts. This gift is far from the perception of Muslims, as they do not talk of true spiritual gifts. There are 20 verses in the Quran that mentions spirit. From these verses, the only thing Muslims know about spirit is that it is a quality of God that is sent to humans God has created. The Muslim tries to tune into the work of the Holy Spirit, and mentions that the spirit God sends gives life, support and strength and that humans have some of God's spirit. On the contrary, the Quran refers to angel Gabriel as *"the Spirit that visited Mary"* (Quran 16:102; 26:192-193). This is in conflict with what the Bible says when the angel Gabriel visited Mary. The Holy Spirit is not an angel nor can He be the angel Gabriel. Rather the angel Gabriel told Mary that the Holy Spirit will come upon her (Luke 1:3 NKJV), which literally means she would conceive by the power of the Holy Spirit.

The Holy Spirit Himself gives life, strength and support to Christians and more than that, the spiritual gift given to the church makes us to function effectively in the body of Christ. Whilst Muslims have no testimonies in their Mosques of the Holy Spirit, for Christians, the Holy Spirit plays a major role in the church of Christ. As it is, no man deserves the gift of God's grace. This leaves no room for self-importance or superiority complex, nor for controversy. In the church of Christ, which is also termed as the body of Christ, the Holy Spirit gives the gifts to every person exactly as He wills. All over the world, the Holy Spirit knows what and where Spirit gifts are needed. He knows what gifts will edify the church most and what gifts can be most effective to reach the world and to minister to the desperate needs of all people. Therefore, the Holy Spirit meets the needs of all believers in their respective calls and localities. In addition, He speaks and sometimes do so directly from person to person (Acts 10:19; 13:2; Hebrews 3:7, Revelation 22:17; John 16:13; Romans 8:26-27; Matthew 10:20; Mark 13:11; Acts 10:19-21 NKJV). For example, Jesus explains how the Holy Spirit will comfort us when we are hurting and bring us peace and help us recall the things we have learnt from God and will not leave us as orphans (John 14:18, 14:26, 27 NKJV). Since the Holy Spirit is the personal presence of Jesus Christ, Jesus informed His disciples, they would not be left helpless or without parental help.

Jesus told His disciples after His resurrection that He would come to those who believe in Him in the person of the Holy Spirit. For the Holy Spirit will help us to tell others about our faith in Jesus Christ. The world lost its opportunity to see Jesus. That was when Jesus mentioned that He would be present in the world for only a short time, and then the world would not see Him "anymore." (That means the next time the world sees Him would be judgement time). Jesus died, arose, lives forever, and dwells in those who believe in Him. If Jesus is living forever and lives within Christian believers, then Christian believers live eternally and become eternal. For they are made eternal by the eternal presence of Christ *within* them. In other words, the Holy Spirit is the very special manifestation of Jesus Christ in Christians. This refers to very special manifestation of the Lord Jesus Christ in the heart of Christians, especially at times when there is a deep awareness of love between the Lord Jesus and those who follow Him (John 14:18–21 NKJV).

Jesus refers to the Holy Spirit as an "another Helper" (John 14:16–17; 16:7 NKJV), who will guide us in our everyday lives. The acceptance of the Holy Spirit is conditional. It means the person who loves Jesus is the one given the Holy Spirit. The Holy Spirit is our Intercessor and therefore is the one who pleads our case. Jesus Christ, however, is our Mediator and Intercessor and makes it possible for us to accept and receive the Holy Spirit. God is the source of the Holy Spirit and He is the one who gave Jesus Christ to the world. He is therefore longing so deeply to give the Holy Spirit to those who love His Son and will do everything He can for them. Therefore, the greatest thing God can do for a person is to give the person His Holy Spirit to live inside him (Luke 11:13 NKJV).

However much the Holy Spirit can do, He cannot do all the work for us. We are still responsible to do our part, especially to consistently read our Bibles and pray, asking the Spirit to show us the truth and teach us how to live. It is important to remember that the Holy Spirit will not prompt us to do anything that goes against the Scriptures. People sometimes justify their actions by saying, *"My conscience told me to do so and so ..."* We need to make sure we are listening to the voice of the Holy Spirit, not the voice of our own desires. In addition, we know which is which by checking this voice against the truth of God's Word.

Now that we have known who the Holy Spirit is, we may have to clarify certain doctrines from the teaching of Islam concerning the Holy Spirit. We have talked about Jesus promising His disciples before He left for heaven, that He would send the Holy Spirit to them. He said to them, "Behold, I send the promise of My Father upon you: but tarry in the city of Jerusalem until you are endued with power from on high" *(Luke 24:49 NKJV)*. Jesus said to His disciples: "However, when the Spirit of truth, has comes, He will guide you into all the truth; for He will not speak on His own authority, but whatever He hears He will speak; and He will tell you things to come" (John 16:13). Jesus continues: *"And I will ask the Father, and He will give you another Counsellor to be with you forever – the Spirit of truth. The world cannot accept Him, because it neither sees Him nor knows Him. But you know Him, for He lives with you and will be in you (John 14:16-17 AMP). In other translations, the Bible records the Holy Spirit as a distinct person: "I will pray the Father, and he shall give you another Comforter, that He may abide with you forever" (John 14:16 KJV). In this context, it reveals that Jesus was speaking of Himself in another form and that the Spirit of Christ rather than Jesus Himself in the flesh. How do Muslims understand this concept of the Holy Spirit in relation to the work Jesus came to do on earth?

Ironically, the Quran states that the mission of Jesus on earth was to take Allah's message to the Jews. The Quran states that Jesus was sent to preach to the Jews and to the world about the coming of Allah's supreme prophet. The Quran calls this supreme prophet *Mohammed*. The Quran explains emphatically that all other men and prophets are beneath Prophet Mohammed. Therefore, in the Islamic view, Jesus is inferior to Mohammed and Muslims believe that the purpose for Jesus' existence was to be a sign of the soon–coming Mohammed (Sura 61:6). We are talking about Jesus who according to the Quran did not die but went to heaven, and now we see Prophet Mohammed is dead and still in his grave. This is about Jesus in the Quran who performed miracles and even raised the dead compared to Mohammed who according to the Quran did no miracle and even confessed that he was a sinner (Quran 40:55, 48:2, and 47:19). Yet the Quran boldly proclaims that Mohammed is greater than Jesus is, and that Jesus was to be the forerunner of Mohammed. What about John the Baptist? Was he not supposed to be the forerunner of Jesus Christ? Is the Quran telling us Mohammed is the soon-coming Holy Spirit that Jesus proclaimed was coming? The writers of the Quran irrationally and blatantly picked passages from the Bible and turned them upside down just to distort facts from the original document, the Bible. That is the unfortunate news for the seekers of the truth.

It is rather unfortunate that educated Muslim scholars, Imams and teachers use these distorted facts to blind the people in the Middle East and the Muslim world, that the Holy Spirit is Prophet Mohammed, the founder of Islam. Many Muslim teachers and Imams erroneously treat the topic on the Holy Spirit to their students. Among them is a renowned Muslim teacher in India whom I have named Dr. Z only to hide his full identity. Dr. Z is a respected teacher among the Muslim folk in India and the Moslem world in general and it is heartbreaking to listen to most of his teachings concerning the Christian Bible. It sounded appalling for a man of such a caliber to use so many lies to lord over his listeners. Dr. Z impresses his listeners with his talent in quoting almost all the verses in the Bible and tells his audience that the Holy Spirit, the third person of the Trinity is Prophet Mohammed. When Jesus told His disciples that He was sending the Holy Spirit to them (John 14:16 NKJV), and that the Holy Spirit will be with the disciples forever, where was Prophet Mohammed? How could Mohammed, born 500 years after Jesus Christ be mentioned or named as a Comforter by Dr. Z? Which kind of comforter was Prophet Mohammed? If Prophet Mohammed, the *"Holy Spirit of the Islamic faith"* were a Comforter, he would not be the type to be involved in war, conquering innocent people and forcing them to accept Islamic faith. The Prophet Muhammed made innocent people weep by forcing Islam on them against their will. Maybe the Islamic scholars have a different definition of what a Comforter is altogether.

The Holy Spirit is said to be with the disciples forever. That was what the Bible says the Holy Spirit is supposed to be doing: *to be with us forever.* Did Prophet Mohammed live forever? The Scripture identifies the Comforter as someone who already dwelt with the disciples: "the Spirit of truth. The world cannot accept him, because it neither sees him nor knows him. But you know him, for he lives with you and will be in you" (John 14:17 NIV). The disciples knew Jesus and that was simply because He dwelt with them. The Bible has already declared Jesus as a Comforter and now, another Comforter is to come. The difference was that the Comforter would soon come to live in them and be with them in a new relationship of spiritual indwelling rather than physical accompaniment. The Holy Spirit will live right inside the disciples of Jesus. That shows that the Holy Spirit is omnipresent, which means He is everywhere and can simply dwell inside a person. Is Prophet Mohammed everywhere and did he live inside the Apostles? When the Holy Spirit came upon Jesus after He was baptized (Luke 3:22; Mathew 3:16 NKJV), was it Prophet Mohammed that descended upon Him?

The Holy Spirit is God and not human and cannot be replaced by mortal man. The Holy Spirit is invisible and cannot be seen, that is why Jesus said of Him, "the Spirit of truth, whom the world cannot receive, because it neither sees Him nor knows Him; but you know Him, for He dwells with you and will be in you" (John 14:17 NKJV). The world saw Prophet Mohammed and knew him as a man. Dr. Z teaches the folks in India that the Spirit of truth is Prophet Mohammed. Was Jesus speaking to Muslims? Is Prophet Mohammed a spirit? Not at all! It is rather unfortunate that a learned person like Dr. Z, together with many other Muslims scholars could deceive many honest and innocent Muslims that the Holy Spirit, the third person of the Trinity is the same as Prophet Mohammed. We have given account of Jesus leaving His disciples and in their sad situation, Jesus encouraged them it was to their advantage that He went back to God, for if He did not go, the Helper who is the Holy Spirit will not come to them. But if He went, He would send Him to them (John 16:7 NKJV). In what way did Prophet Mohammed help the disciples of Jesus Christ and His followers? Muslim teachers and imams think the Holy Spirit is a man; for they do not know Him neither understand who He is. It is therefore a blunder on their part to call Prophet Mohammed the *"Spirit of truth"* whom Jesus said would guide us into all truth. This simply does not click nor fit together, for it is unimportant. Muslims do not accept the most important concept of Christianity based on the death and resurrection of Jesus Christ; how then could Muslims build a wall of untruth around the Holy Spirit sent by Jesus Christ?

The moment Muslims refused to accept the central message of Jesus Christ concerning His death and resurrection, discussion about the Holy Spirit who is also called the Spirit of Christ has to be discarded and thrown into the bin. How could such a sensitive issue be taken so lightly by calling the Holy Spirit Prophet Mohammed? The Scriptures says before Jesus ascended into heaven, He promised to send the Holy Spirit to the world. The Scripture categorically states that whilst Jesus was ascending into heaven His disciples witnessed the (Acts 1:9-12 NKJV) moment that He was taken up. What happened after Jesus ascended? Did Prophet Mohammed descend from heaven right after Jesus left the earth? Who witnessed that? If Prophet Mohammed is the Spirit of truth that Jesus was sending, the moment Jesus went to heaven, Prophet Mohammed was supposed to have come down from heaven to replace Jesus. Logically, he was supposed to have first come to the disciples of Jesus just as the Holy Spirit actually did. We know from the Scriptures that the Holy Spirit (whom the Muslims believe to be Prophet Mohammed) came *10 days* after Jesus had left for Heaven. There was no time to wait as Jesus did not want to leave them behind like orphans (John 14:18 NKJV). The Holy Spirit came on the day of Pentecost by the time the disciples were together in the Upper Room (Acts 2:1-4 NKJV). Was Mohammed born *10 days* after Jesus went to heaven? The Holy Spirit is mention in the Bible *352* time; *264* times in the New Testament and *88* times in the Old Testament. If the Holy Spirit has a name just like Jesus has a name in the Quran, let Muslim scholars show which pages in the Bible that mention or refer to the name of Prophet Mohammed as the Holy Spirit. It is with much enthusiasm that Muslims accept the doctrines of the entire Bible and even though some believe the Bible to be corrupted, still they find it important to relate everything in the Quran to the Bible. It is unfortunate one cannot find a single reference that Christian scholars and apologists make of the contents of the Bible in reference to the Quran. The Quran should have found its original source in itself to authenticate the true message concerning Jesus Christ. It should not in any way justify its own interpretation through the Bible. It claims the Bible to be the true original source. It should therefore be proper that whatever the Quran says in reference to the Bible be not in contradiction. The original source of the Bible is the Holy Spirit Himself. It is the Holy Spirit who inspired and motivated men of God to write the Bible (2 Timothy 3:16-17 NKJV) and though it has gone through several translation, it still contains the authentic message to prove its validity.

The Holy Spirit according to Jesus will teach the disciples all things and remind them of all that Jesus has said. The Prophet Mohammed never believed that Jesus died and resurrected; how could he relate himself to the sayings of Jesus who spoke directly to His disciples and the Christian generation yet to be born? Did the Prophet Mohammed know all things, and did he perform miracles? Miracles are different from magic. True Christians are led by the Holy Spirit perform miracles and do not do magic. When we witness miracles, signs, and wonders in our churches and crusades held around the world, Muslims scholars wonder where the power for those miracles come from. I sent a video clip of healing and miracle crusade of Pastor Benny Hinn to a Muslim friend of mine who after viewing it said it was a nice film. Then I sent another clip of Prophet T. B Joshua of the Synagogue of All Nations performing mighty miracles in the name of Jesus, and my Muslim friend could not comprehend it. There was no absolute difference between the miracles that took place at Pastor Benny Hinn's crusade and that of Prophet T.B. Joshua in Mexico; both being led by the Holy Spirit. At the crusade of Prophet T. B. Joshua, those possessed by demons were set free and many sicknesses including those sitting on wheelchairs got healed. What took place was so incredible and spectacular that anyone that witnessed this would conclude that was the hand of God.

These are miracles done in the name of Jesus by the power of the Holy Spirit. Many Muslims have not yet come to the full knowledge of the work of the Holy Spirit on earth and have not understood His role as the representative of Jesus Christ in the world. The Holy Spirit will be with Christians forever and the time He leaves the earth is when Christ Jesus returns to bring judgment to the world. How could we relate the Holy Spirit to Prophet Mohammed who was born 600 years after Jesus had gone to heaven and never lived even up to 100 years but died? Jesus said the Holy Spirit will be with us forever (John 14:16 NKJV). The Holy Spirit is still in the world today, but Prophet Mohammed remains in the grave. To make much more ado about this, Muslims surprisingly believe that Jesus is still alive today.

There are examples of people who are supposed to know better but rather live in ignorance and dilute the gospel of Jesus Christ. Dr. Z., the renowned Muslim scholar try to prove to know the Bible better than the Christians. He displays much arrogance in his knowledge but looks quite timid to accept the truth written on the wall about the Holy Spirit. The next terrible comment he makes affirms that Jesus Christ was a Muslim. Was Jesus truly a Moslem? Can't this be ridiculous? If Jesus was a Muslim, why are Muslims killing Christians, the followers of Jesus? Why are Moslems burning churches in Nigeria? If Jesus was a Muslim why is Boka Haram, a set of radical Muslims, bombing Christian schools, burning Bibles and kidnapping Christian girls? There was a record of 276 Christian girls kidnapped in April 15, 2014 in Nigerian by Boka Haram. If Jesus was a Muslim, why should Isis kill and cut of the heads of those who confessed Jesus Christ? I thought the Quran says Jesus was very compassionate and full of love and that this same Jesus told us to love our enemies and pray for those who treat us badly. If Jesus was a Muslim, then Muslims should start to teach their children that Jesus was a good Muslim, and that everyone who worship Jesus or call upon His name should receive equally treatment like any other Muslim. Jesus said to the Jews, "I have spoken to you of earthly things and you do not believe; how then will you believe if I speak of heavenly things? (John 3:1, 2, 11, 12 NIV). Jesus taught that we are to be completely changed and be born from above, from God and not of the earth. Jesus repeated the importance of being born again, that unless a man is born again, he cannot enter into the Kingdom of God. To be born again is the work of the Holy Spirit. Jesus illustrated the point by picturing the wind. The Spirit of God works just like the wind. We may not know how the wind works, but we can see the effect. It is so with the Holy Spirit: we may not know how He works, but we can see the effects. For a man to be born again is a spiritual process. It has nothing to do with the natural. If Muslims have not the Holy Spirit, how could they be born of the Spirit? Anyone born of the Spirit believes that Jesus Christ died and resurrected from the death. Jesus said to the Jews "Whoever believes in him is not condemned, but whoever does not believe stands condemned already because they have not believed in the name of God's one and only Son" (John 3:18 NIV). A person who does not believe that Jesus died for his sins already stands guilty of all sins committed. That person is already condemned and is because the person has rejected the great remedy for man's sins, which is Christ Jesus. Therefore, unbelief leading to rejecting and refusing Jesus Christ as the resurrected Son of God is the greatest condemnation man can experience. That is why Muslims like Dr. Z and others are to put away their pride and worldly knowledge, to teach their children about the truth concerning Jesus Christ. Christians are reaching out to Moslems all over the world and bringing salvation to their doors. That is because it is the greatest command that came directly from Jesus (Mark 16:15- 16; Mathew 29:19 NKJV).

Jesus loves Muslims so much that His heart bleeds for their sake and lo and behold many Muslims have had a personal encounter with Jesus Christ and have experienced revival in their lives. There are many wonderful lovely Muslims who really want to serve God, but unless they accept Jesus Christ as their Savior, they will be far away from serving the true God. Unfortunately, out there are also wonderful loving Muslims, who have been blinded by greedy teachers that call themselves Imams and men of God, but in their hearts are only nursing corruption against their own people. They can wake up from spiritual blindness and come to Jesus. How could the type like Dr. Z and many of our Muslim brothers understand heavenly things if they cannot simply practice what Jesus says; that irrespective of what religion a person belongs to, no one must die because of his or her faith or ideology. If Dr. Z believes Jesus was a Muslim, then he should stand up against what other Muslims are doing against Christians and not only Christians but against all people they name as infidels or unbelievers.

Jesus Christ whom Dr. Z claims is a Muslim is compassionate and by His Holy Spirit calls for all to come to full repentance. The type of Dr. Z is not only found in India but also all across the world. People who cannot decipher the truth from evidence and delight in holding their audience to ransom with deception can find it difficult to understand the way the Holy Spirit operates. The audience of Dr. Z enjoy the air of superiority surrounding their learned Imam. He has a method and style he uses to win people into the Islamic faith that create resistance against those who try to challenge him. Together with his audience blinded by false doctrine, they laugh and mock at Christians who ask questions about Jesus. In a very deceptive manner, Dr. Z always ask Christians who ask questions, *"if I answer you, would you like to become a Muslim"?* The Bible mentions how many false prophets and teachers will appear and deceive many people (Mathew 24:11 NKJV) and we are warned of people like Dr. Z of India. The Bible again warns, "Watch out for false prophets. They come to you in sheep's clothing, but inwardly they are ferocious wolves" (Mathew 7:15 NIV). Jesus is still alive, but Mohammed is not. Not only is Mohammed not alive, but Buddha, Confucius, Zoroaster, Joseph Smith, etc. are all dead, but only Jesus lives forever and so is His Holy Spirit who lives and occupies the life of every child of God who has Christ Jesus as Lord and Savior.

7. The Historical Jesus, The Christ and the Word of God

Among all the great men and women in the world, one can clearly see that Jesus Christ has become the center of attention in history. There are mysteries and indefinable characteristics that sets Him apart from other human beings and His personality captivated those who heard Him speak. Jesus of Nazareth (*Jeshua Hamashiach*), whom Pilate regarded as the King of the Jews was different from all other men in history. Jesus was brought up in a comparatively insignificant village called Nazareth. "Can anything good come out of Nazareth?" (John 1:46), asked Nathanael, who later became one of Jesus` disciples. What is peculiar about Him is that, He lived in the time when no mass media existed. Just think about carnal men knowing the identity of Jesus by the color of His skin, hair and the form of His complete humanity. That would not have been quite ideal for God, the Creator of the universe in human form. No doubt He came to the world at the time when there was no television, no photography, no newspaper and no printing press. It is not surprise therefore that almost nothing was written and preserved of His ministry and no wonder there is no first century inscription to Him or no mention of His name by His immediate contemporaries. Jesus Himself never wrote a book and did not owe property or even led a political party and ministered entirely outside the established religious framework. Yet his greatness has attracted and baffled every human being on earth.

Many ideas and thoughts in circulation including those of people who call themselves the *"Commonsense Family"* advocate that Jesus never lived. There are skeptics that also say there was no secular evidence that Jesus ever existed and that the Bible is only a collection of stories and fables and a living Jesus was just a figment of the imagination of Christians. How could a book like the Bible, so revealing and appealing beyond the scope of human imagination be classified as a figment of someone's imagination? That makes this topic relevant to write home about, for it is not a question of whether Jesus lived or not, but what is the intention of skeptics. Actually, the skeptics have chosen their own destiny and will have nothing to do with a righteous and holy man like Jesus. The skeptics, just like the atheists detest the work of the cross and the fact that Jesus came to save them from the sins they love so much to commit. They have never been happy about Jesus coming into the world. When Jesus died, the 19th century atheist and philosopher by name Friederich Nietzsche coined the phrase "God is dead" and in his book, *"The AntiChrist"*, Nietzsche said of Jesus: "He died too early; he himself would have revoked his doctrine had he reached greater maturity". Both Nietzsche and Adolf Hitler of Germany wished that Jesus had never been born. Others share this sentiment. Among such is Ellen Johnsen, the president of American Atheists who said on CNN TV in an interview with Larry King, that "There is not one shred of secular evidence that there was a Jesus Christ". There is also conspiracy theory made against Jesus by Dan Brown who authored Da Vinci Code. Da Vinci portrayed a new Jesus in his book and said Jesus had a secret marriage with Mary Magdalene. He believed that there was a Jesus; for if he did not, he wouldn't have chosen to write something contrary to the identity of the true Jesus. The Bible has ever existed before Ellen Johnsen and Dan Brown were born and it bears concrete evidences about the historical Jesus.

Far from that, Muslim and some Jewish scholars say that the Bible is full of contradictions.

There are no contradictions in the Bible which as divine revelation is inerrant. All apparent discrepancies are in reality due to the insufficient interpretive ability of readers and Bible students. The problem lies not with the Word of God but with our understanding which is limited. Interestingly, it is Christianity that bridged the gap between the Jews and pagans who came to know God and it was the word of God in the Bible that saved the pagans. Therefore, there is no contradictions in the entirety of the Bible as thought. One may see instances of different wording that may seem to be apparent contradiction in the gospel of Mathew, Mark and John. However, they all write and describe the same or similar events in detail though in different styles and with different emphases. That makes the credentials about Jesus so unique and palpable to human understanding. It is impossible to talk about the Bible as the Word of God without speaking about its inerrancy and infallibility. The inerrancy means the Bible was written free from mistakes or errors. The Spirit of God guided holy men of God to write what God intended them to write. The events and occurrences found in the Bible are not fictitious of anyone's imagination but were true occurrences and rightfully recorded. In the New Testament where we find the four Gospels, we come across hundreds of references about Jesus Christ. There are those who date the writing of the Gospels to the second century A.D., more than 100 years after Jesus death. The great majority of scholars will also grant that the Epistles of Paul were written by Paul in the middle of the first century A.D., less than 40 years after the death of Jesus Christ. Unless we believe what the writers of the New Testament said about Jesus, we cannot know exactly what Jesus did, what He said and what He stood for. Nor can we fathom the wonderful gifts that He offered to humans on earth. Should we believe in the Bible or not? Should we care whether Jesus is God, man or He was just a myth?

Whilst many have tried to disprove the content of the Bible and the historical Jesus, there have been numerous archaeological findings that evidence the life of Jesus Christ on earth. These evidences can be so much that they cannot even find space in this book. Since men who lived and bore witnesses to all that occurred among the Jewish people wrote the Bible, the same is true of those who bore eyewitness accounts about the historical Jesus. There were evidences of more than 30 gospels written by men of trust, but most of them were not included in the Bible due to unknown or unreliable authorship. The lost ones and those not chosen due to political reasons were preserved in the four gospels which historians called the source. Historians therefore have to rely on interpretations of the four Gospels in the Bible, mostly written several decades after the death of Jesus. One of the gospels that Muslims normally use because it deviates from the true gospel is that of Barnabas. Muslims are not able to distinguish between the Gospel of Barnabas and the Epistle of Barnabas. The Gospel of Barnabas supports some of the things in the Quran and at the same time contradicts it, whilst the Epistle of Barnabas tells exactly about the death and resurrection of Jesus as told in the Bible. These two books are not included in the Bible.

Biblical scholars and historians from the earliest years of the Christian era have debated the historical existence of Jesus. The evidence that Jesus existed is persuasive to the vast majority of scholars, whether Christians or non-Christians. Jesus Christ happens to be the most famous man that ever lived. How do we know? Most theological historians, archaeologists, Christians and non-Christians alike, believe that Jesus really did walk the Earth. Most of them drew their conclusion from the textual evidence in the Bible. There are other confirmations that also bear evidence that Jesus Christ existed. The Bible says that God by His Spirit bears witness of Jesus Christ (John 15:26 NKJV) and convinces the world concerning Him (John 16:8-11 NKJV). It is therefore possible for someone without knowledge about ancient historical writings to believe that Jesus did live.

Historians and archaeologists have determined that the biography about Jesus Christ as written by the Gospel writers is reliable. All the Gospel writers report to a large extent the same facts about Jesus Christ. Because of the accuracy of the gospels, any knowledgeable person with discerning spirit will agree with the authors. Mathew and John who personally travelled with Jesus for over three years bear witness about Jesus in their gospels. The other two gospels were written by Mark and Luke, these two being close associates of the apostles. They had to rely on testimonies about the life of Jesus. Luke stated he gathered the material for his account of Jesus' life from *"eyewitnesses"* (Luke 1:2 KJV). The Gospels were therefore recorded from eyewitness accounts of Jesus' life, death, burial and Jesus' resurrection. Matthew and John were eyewitnesses and Peter likely provided John Mark with much of his material. In the olden days, eyewitnesses played important role in sending information across, and was predominantly handed over as oral tradition from generation to generation. There was no doubt an input from Paul, who was instructed by the resurrected Christ (Galatians 1:11–12 KJV). The four Gospel writers had direct access to the facts they were re-cording and the early church accepted these four gospels since they agreed with what was known about the life of Jesus. The descriptions about the factual events are unique to each author, and the facts are largely in agreement.

There were eyewitnesses of the life of Christ and the Bible mentions there were over 500 people that saw Jesus after His resurrection. The Apostle Paul had to quash rumors in the Corinthian congregation that Jesus Christ had never been resurrected. That made Paul to meet some of the people who saw Jesus after He resurrected and talked with them personally. Paul named some of the eyewitnesses who had been with the resurrected Christ (1 Corinthians 15:5–8 NKJV). An instance was after Peter had failed the Lord Jesus Christ miserably and denied knowing Him at the critical hour of His death, Peter was covered with shame until Jesus personally met him after His resurrection. Jesus to assure Peter of His forgiveness and love asked him three times if he loves Him. Peter had a forceful testimony, for he had personally experienced the historical Jesus and could readily testify after the resurrection that Jesus is Lord overall. In the Acts of the Apostle and Paul's letters, it is evident that many people were alive who could have disputed the facts provided by the New Testament writers if the details were wrong. Instead, there is agreement and consistency in what we are told. Former persecutors and detractors like Paul (previously Saul) did not dispute the records. In fact, his encounter with Jesus on his way to Damascus to persecute Christians before his conversion made him one of the greatest witnesses about the living Jesus. In addition, Christians in the era of the Roman Empire were willing to live under the constant threat of death, which would have been unthinkable unless they were convinced that Jesus was not a charlatan.

There are also historical writings other than the biblical record that proves that Jesus really did live. Tacitus and Josephus, and other ancient writers such as Suetonius, Thallus, Pliny the Younger, Julius Africanus, and Lucian, all historians recorded the existence of Jesus Christ. Suetonius, chief secretary to Emperor Hadrian wrote: *"there was a man named Christ who lived during the first century"*. Quoting from the Jewish Talmud (collection of Jewish doctrines and laws), it states, *"we learn that Jesus was conceived out of wedlock, gathered disciples, made blasphemous claims about himself, and worked miracles, but these miracles are attributed to sorcery and not of God"*. The conception of Jesus without an earthly father might have given rise to the controversy in His days; no wonder the Jewish Talmud states: *"He was conceived out of wedlock"*. These are tangible references and most important factors worthy to consider among ancient historians that were focused on political and military leaders, and not on obscure rabbis from distant provinces of the Roman Empire. Ancient historians among them Jews, Greeks and Romans confirm the major events that present themselves in the New Testament, even though they were not believers themselves. In one page of his final works entitled Annals (written ca. AD 116, book 15, and chapter 44), the Roman historian and Senator Tacitus (A.D. 55-120) referred to Christ and mentioned his execution by Pontius Pilate in the reign of Tiberius and the existence of the early Christians. Senator Tacitus is considered to be one of the greatest historians in the first century Rome, and he mentioned about *superstitious Christians* and wrote of Nero who tortured Christians and that the Christians were hated for their enormities. Scholars generally consider Tacitus reference to the execution of Jesus by

Pontius Pilate to be both authentic and non-Christian evidence, and of historical value as an independent Roman source. According to Historian Ronald Mollor, the Annals is *Tacitus crowning achievement* which represents the *pinnacle of Roman historical writing.*

Another important source is Flavius Josephus, a famous pro-Roman Jew historian, (A.D. 38-100), associated with Emperor Titus, in his published lengthy history of the *Jewish Antiquities,* (Book 18, ch.3, par.3), and discussed the period that the Jews were governed by Pontius Pilate. He mentioned that *"Jesus was a wise man who did surprising feats, taught many people and had many followers from among the Greeks and Jews and that He was believed to be the Messiah, accused by the Jewish leaders who condemned Him to be crucified by Pilate, and was considered to be resurrected".* He refers to James, *the brother of Jesus,* in his Antiquities. In verse 18:3 he writes, *"Now there was about this time Jesus, a wise man, if it be lawful to call Him a man. For he was one who wrought surprising feats ... He was Christ and appeared to them alive again the third day, as the divine prophets had foretold these and ten thousand other wonderful things concerning him".* One version reads, *"At this time there was a wise man named Jesus. His conduct was good, and he was known to be virtuous. Many people from among the Jews and the other nations became his disciples but those who became his disciples did not abandon his discipleship. They reported that he had appeared to them three days after his crucifixion, and that he was alive; accordingly, he was perhaps the Messiah concerning whom the prophets have recounted wonders."* The Jewish Antiquities of Josephus was based on the translation of Louis H. Feldman, a professor at Yeshiva University.

On the account of the crucifixion as stated in Luke 23:44-45 NKJV, Thallus (ca AD 52) wrote *"on the whole world there pressed a most fearful darkness; and the rocks were rent by an earthquake, and many places in Judea and other districts were thrown down".* This darkness, Thallus in the third book of his History, records that it appeared to him, to be an eclipse of the sun. Julius Africanus quotes the historian Thallus in a discussion of the darkness, which followed the crucifixion of Christ. Julius Africanus concluded in his Extant Writings, that Thallus *mentioning of the eclipse was describing the one at*

Jesus crucifixion. The reason Africanus doubted the eclipse is because Easter happens near the full moon and a solar eclipse would have been impossible at that time, as was well known. However, modern scholars see the darkness as a literary creation rather than a historical event. Presumably, Africanus conclusion was right since he describes exactly what the Bible describes which was of no coincidence, for this had to do with the resurrection of Jesus Christ. There was also Pliny the Younger who in his *Letters 10:96,* recorded that there were Christians worship practices including the fact that Christians worshipped Jesus as God and were very ethical, and he includes a reference to the love feast and Lord Supper. The work of Lucian (circa 120–after 180), a Greek writer and rhetorician also reveals the work of Jesus Christ on earth and this is what he said, *"The Christians, you know, worship a man to this day the distinguished personage who introduced their novel rites, and was crucified on that account. . . . . You see, these misguided creatures start with the general conviction that they are immortal for all time, which explains the contempt of death and voluntary self-devotion which are so common among them; and then it was impressed on them by their original lawgiver that they are all brothers, from the moment that they are converted, and deny the gods of Greece, and worship the crucified sage, and live after his laws. All this they take quite on faith, with the result that they despise all worldly goods alike, regarding them merely as common property."* Though Lucian opposed Christianity, he acknowledged Jesus, and believed that Jesus was crucified, and that the Christians worship Him and that this was done by faith.

The Talmud cited the crucifixion of Jesus by saying that *"On the eve of the Passover Yeshua was hanged. For forty days before the execution took place, a herald went forth and cried, "He is going forth to be stoned because he has practiced sorcery and enticed Israel to apostasy. Anyone who can say anything in his favor let him come forward and plead on his behalf." But since nothing was brought forward in his favor he was hanged on the eve of the Passover!"* The Talmud is a huge collection of doctrines and laws compiled and written before the 8th Century, A.D., by ancient Jewish teachers. The works are considered important by some Christians because they believe them to confirm the historical

Jesus and provides a non-Christian validation of the Gospel accounts. There could be more eyewitnesses in A.D. 70, the entire city was burnt to the ground and it should not be surprised that many of the eyewitnesses of Jesus were killed and much evidence about Jesus destroyed. On this account, historians both favorable and unfavorable regarding Jesus did write about him.

In our modern world today, there are so many conceptions that opinion leaders hold about the historical Jesus. The Jews say He is a man just like any ordinary person. They believe that Jesus is a founder of a new religion, even though Jesus had told them He did not come to destroy the law in the Torah but rather came to fulfill it (Mathew 5:17 NKJV). Others claim Jesus to be a postmodern Jew who came to offer something that was sensational rather than noble and caused a change that was meant to affect negatively the Jewish faith. Some of the things that Jesus taught were considered to be contrary to the Jewish faith, which made the Jews skeptical and unwilling to accept Jesus as a man sent by God to save them. The Christian faith preaches that Jesus Christ is the Son of God and that He is God, the second person of the Holy Trinity. There are however some Christian liberals who question the deity of Jesus Christ as the Son of God and God at the same time. There are also certain non-Christians elements who believe that Jesus was an important prophet and a wise man, but they do not think He was divine enough to be called the Son of God. The Hindu's and Buddhists say Jesus is a Wiseman that once upon a time lived on earth. Muslims say they love Jesus and believe He had miraculous birth and that He was born through the will of God, without an earthly father and without sexual act. On the other hand, Muslims place Jesus in the same class as Adam; for they say: *just as Adam was created without a mother or father so is Jesus, and that He is only a mere human created by God like Adam.* They believe in miracles performed by Jesus but that those miracles they said were done under the permission of Allah. The Muslims assert that Jesus was a great prophet of God. Muslims and Jews in general do not believe that Jesus is the Son of God; neither do they believe that He is God. We cannot ascribe any blame to Muslims and Jews for not believing in Jesus Christ as God's Son. The acceptance of such divine responsibility is solely attributed to religious view.

There is a spirit in religion like an opium which when it hangs on the neck of a person, can lead to spiritual blindness and be suicidal to a person's salvation. Religion has caused more harm than good at various times and in various places and this stems from religious intolerance. We see even today this phenomenon among religious fundamentalists. That includes also some Christians who have no understanding of the love of God and how God is yearning for us to live together in peace with each other. Others also mention Jesus had some good ideas, but not enough to be the Son of God. Still there are those who also speak of Jesus as a historical figure but do not recognize Him the way other religions portray Him and so do not believe in anything about Jesus. Labels of all kinds are also used to describe who Jesus is. Some say He is a deacon or a servant of God. Others say He is a priest and a bishop. Many say He is a shepherd, a good friend of the poor and some say He is a king. To some people Jesus was a rabbi, a healer and a teacher with some peculiar power. All the above definitions of who Jesus is sound quite impressive for a person every society acknowledges and places so high. There is therefore no doubt that Jesus is a unique person in history.

Former Cambridge professor and skeptic, C.S. Lewis after he had carefully examined the life of Jesus, had his life completely changed. Jesus might have been a controversial person and His records and lifestyle baffle many of the great thinkers of history. The atheists also say it loud on the rooftop, *"God does not exist"* and they scoff at the idea of Jesus Christ being the Son of God and at the same time be a man. Sadly enough, atheists mock at the virgin birth of Jesus and call Him a bastard, that He was born out of wedlock and had no father. Atheism as most of us will admit is a folly. For atheists see there is a world that could not make itself, and yet they will not believe there is a God that made it. Atheists are without any excuse on the Day of Judgment, as the god of this world has blinded their minds (2 Corinthians 4:4 NKJV). There are others who like Mahatma Gandhi spoke highly of the righteousness of Jesus

Christ and concluded He had the most profound words (1955). On the contrary, Gandhi separated Jesus' teaching on ethics from His personal claim as Saviour and only believed He was simply a great man who taught lofty moral principles. More to this was American Founding Father, President Thomas Jefferson's memorable words in the Declaration of the American Independence. These words were rooted in Jesus' teaching of human equality, that all men are created equal. Besides, all the other great men of history who had a great number of followers wooed their followers and won them over to follow their teaching by their charisma. Most of these men lived a lifestyle which did not reflect their messages. On the other hand, Jesus taught, expounded and proclaimed a message that was identical with the way he lived. Jesus did what none of them could do and that was to forgive sins, something only God could do.

Coming to the world of art, many great artists have also tried to imagine and depict what Jesus looks like during His life on earth. Master painters like Rembrandt, Leonardo da Vinci, Raphael, Durer and Michelangelo devoted their lives and focused their genius upon portraying the Master Jesus. Churches and museums in many countries display wonderful works by innumerable artists about how Jesus looks like. Many have painted the baby Jesus with His mother or on a manger bed, surrounded by his parents, the stable animals, and those who came to celebrate His birth by worshipping Him. Others have depicted Him in the Temple at age 12, puzzling the learned scholars with His knowledge about God and His spiritual wisdom. Perhaps a favorite work of art, illustrating some dramatic scenes from the Gospel accounts of Jesus' life and ministry; loving the children, feeding the multitudes, healing the sick, teaching His disciples will do much more to portray the Jesus of history. So many have tried to capture a glimpse of Jesus and some of the portraits they display are masterpieces, others of much more modest value. One can easily be moved and blessed by these pictures, especially those showing Christ travailing in the Garden of Gethsemane, enduring the tortures of His trial, and weeping for the world from the cross of Calvary. It is even more inspiring looking at the paintings of the resurrected Savior and

His Transfiguration. Awesome indeed is Michelangelo's monumental paintings on the ceiling of the Sistine Chapel in the Vatican. Equally marvelous is da Vinci's famous masterpiece, *The Last Supper.* All these are glamorous memories of the historical Jesus.

We thank God for all the artists and how many of them have portrayed the historical Jesus. They are very much appreciated. These remarkable works can make awaken in many of us a desire for something more. Oh! how many of us longed to see Jesus for ourselves? One cannot tell how many times some of us have tried to go back in history and visualize the scene of Jesus' birth. Only Joseph and Mary were there when He came to the world. The rest of the world was asleep. As Mary held Him and looked into His face for the first time, one may wonder if she realized she was touching the infant God. There must have been something special about the way He looked. I have many times mentioned how fortunate the Apostles were to have been with Jesus, touching him, ate with Him and listened to Him as a person. It does not seem ordinary for me to have that opportunity as an ordinary human being to see God on earth with my own naked eyes sleeping in the same room with Him. It was just an honor for the Apostles. Humanly speaking, the mere thought of Jesus being God and man sounds quite unreasonable to most of the people in the world. In principle, it may sound unreasonable and illogic, but one cannot assume illogic and unreasonableness in things pertaining to God. Moreover, the wisdom of God is different from the wisdom of man, for as the heavens are higher than the earth, so are God's ways higher than man's ways and God's thoughts higher than man's thoughts (Isaiah 55:9 NKJV). Therefore, since there are different conceptions about who Jesus is, there appears to be a mystery surrounding the issue of who Jesus really is. However, the most important question is: Who is Jesus to you and what do you personally say about Him?

There are various accounts given in both the New and Old Testament leading to possible conclusions about who Jesus really is. The life of Jesus Christ as prophesied in the Old Testament is revealed in the New Testament. The New Testament is the new covenant between humankind and God, and the grace bestowed upon man that was revealed through Jesus Christ, the Son of God. Some of the books in the Bible which most clearly reveal who Jesus Christ is include the Gospels, Acts of the Apostles, the Epistles, and the book of Revelation. However, it must be stressed that the Bible in its entirety from cover to cover reveals who Jesus Christ actually is. The true revelation of Jesus Christ to humanity is the work of the Spirit of the living God and it is my prayer that the content of this book may be a blessing to you.

There are many scholars of the Bible including Jewish and Muslim scholars, who think Jesus never claimed to be the Messiah. On the other hand, there are many others who feel that He actually did. The Bible describes Jesus Christ as the Messiah, the savior of humanity. In the book of Mark, Jesus happened to be in the neighborhood of Caesarea Philippi, a city north of the Sea of Galilee, and Jesus asked his disciples, "*Who do men say that I am?*" They gave various answers: John the Baptist, Elijah, or another of the prophets. Then Jesus asked them, "But who do you say that I am?" And Peter formerly called Simon answered, "You are the Christ, the Son of the Living God." Jesus then replied, "Flesh and blood has not revealed this to you, but my Father who is in heaven" (Mathew 16:17 NKJV). Peter was convinced beyond reasonable doubt that Jesus is the Christ, the Son of the living God. It is only God who can convict the soul of a man, lead him to personally trust and believe that Jesus Christ is the Son of the Living God. This is because man is only flesh and blood. For a man to believe in Jesus as God's Son, he should be led by the Spirit of God. After Peter had made such confession, Jesus told His disciples not to tell anybody until the appointed time has come. Why, if He accepted the designation, did He want it to be kept secret? One persuasive answer often given is that Jesus was radically revising the traditional idea of the Messiah. If the people thought He was the promised Messiah, they would demand that He lives up to their expectations by being forced to become their king. Jesus actually had no intention of meeting the expectation of people by becoming a conquering king.

Whilst the Jewish people were under the rule of the Roman Empire, they had for generations hoped and waited for a Messiah prophesied to be a Jewish deliverer. They had been waiting patiently for such a deliverer, who was also termed as the Messiah, with the title of a King; the heir to the throne of David; to come and take them from the sufferings of the Roman oppression. Their hope was that this promised Messiah, also a King, would overthrow the Roman Empire, and re-establish a glorious kingdom like the kingdom of the olden days to promote justice and righteousness. This coming King, known to be the Divine Messiah; would come as a Savior and would bring about a radical transformation of life that would meet their expectations and affect their livelihood. Unfortunately, the one that came was different. For even though He lived among them, He did not intend to become the conquering king they expected. He was not in position to satisfy their expectation to help them overthrow the rule of the Roman Empire and thus establish an earthly kingdom. What the people saw was rather a herald of the kingdom of God who was radically revising the traditional ideas of the prophesied Messiah and bringing transformation that was very alien to their method of teachings. The Elders and the Scribes found it difficult to associate with Him, for His was not of an earthly Kingdom but certainly of a kingdom outside the domain of men, which of course is of God, the One He called His Father.

Questioning His new ways of teachings and the impact He had on the Jewish tradition, this Promised Messiah only talked about God and His Kingdom, for it was vivid that He did have some special relationship to the kingdom He was preaching about. Simply those who heard Him preached about the Kingdom of God were frequently perplexed, and in most cases, they found Him modest and humble in His method of approach to life and nature. He claimed He was God's Son on earth, but He never claimed superiority over the people as the Son of God. One thing He did in humility was to turn the people's hearts from Himself to God, whilst He made Himself unequal with or lower than God. There were also certain times He expected them to know who He actually was, leaving that for the people themselves to judge and to find out for themselves. At other times, He astonished people by challenging the authority of the scholars of His days. He even appeared to question the authority of the Hebrew Bible with His new teachings. He was so audacious with the authority to forgive sins, even though the people said that only God could do that.

Apart from the above observations about the person of Jesus, He happened also to be just a unique person and a disturbing figure to unclean spirits and demons. He was so mighty that His presence alone had an impact upon evil spirits. There were other instances where demons were so much troubled by His presence and what they could only do was to reveal His identity. Whenever the unclean spirits saw Him, they would fall down before Him and shout, *"You are the Son of God!"* (Mark 3:11 NKJV). They knew who He was, and they were troubled of His very presence and afraid that He might cast them into hell before their time. The atmosphere surrounding Him was so charged with power, healing, and anointing that everybody wanted to catch a glimpse of Him. As the crowd tried to push forward to touch Him, hoping that they would get help, the evil spirits, on the other hand, bowed to him or fled from him, stricken by His deity. They fell down not because of any other reason, but because they acknowledged Him to be the Christ, the Son of the living God (Luke 4:41 NKJV). By rebuking them, Jesus would not allow them to speak, and so they were silent in their fear. The unclean spirits are demonic powers that possessed innocent victims and tortured them for years. There were so many of them during the time of Jesus. Jesus full of compassion and mercy set the victims free by driving away the evil spirits from them.

Despite His popularity, Jesus was not accepted by His own people, not until after His resurrection (John 7:5 NKJV). It was difficult for those from His own hometown of Nazareth to accept Him. At the end, when they had witnessed His resurrection, they came to believe that He was the Son of God and not actually the Son of Joseph, the husband of His earthily mother (Acts 1:14 NKJV). The family of Jesus and many others bore witness to the mighty works He did, and they came to understand that He was no ordinary being. They saw the hand of God upon Him and to some of them, the plan of God was about to be revealed to humans through Jesus Christ.

From this account of history, we have understood that Jesus Christ is a member of the Godhead known as the Trinity. The history of Jesus is therefore linked to God, the Father of all creation. This is because the Bible affirms that "All things were made by him" (John 1:3 NKJV) and for Him were all things created, that are in heaven, and that are in earth, visible and invisible, whether they be thrones, or dominions, or principalities, or powers, all things were created by Him, and for Him (Colossians 1:16 NKJV). Jesus stepped into creation with the Father (*Elohim*) in Genesis, to create the universe, and it was by Him that the worlds were made (Hebrews 1:2). Jesus, the second person of the Elohim, made His preexistence known to the Jews that Moses wrote about Him (John 5:46 NKJV). They did not understand Him and accused Him of lying and even stated that they knew His father to be Joseph the Carpenter. He delved back hundred years to the first five books of the Bible, called *The Pentateuch,* and told them in plain language of how Moses mentioned Him. He referred to their Law that He was the Lord their God who brought them out of Egypt (Exodus 20:2: Deuteronomy 5:6 NKJV). To provoke the Jews even the more about his preexistence, He said to them, that their Father Abraham rejoiced by seeing His day (John 8:56 NKJV) and that before Abraham came to existence, He is (John 8:48-59 NKJV). The Jews said that Jesus was not even 50 years old (verse 57), so how could He argue that Abraham saw Him on the earth? Yes! Indeed, Abraham saw the day of the Lord by faith. The Jews simply failed to grasp that the promises were made to Abraham before the nation of Israel was even born. Abraham experienced Jesus when he was told to offer his son Isaac as sacrifice.

Jesus Christ is mentioned in the Scripture as the only mediator between man and God. The historical Jesus therefore reconciles all men to God through the power of the Holy Spirit. He is absolutely the only one who is able to show the world how God looks like and to bring the world back to God. From the time of creation when sin engrossed the world, humanity forgot God their Creator and it became worse at the time of Noah when men had no more honor for God. The only solution for man to avoid going astray was for God to reveal Himself and be reconciled to the world. In order that man could be reconciled to God, who is the Father of all humanity, Jesus assumed human flesh to pave the way for man. The historical Jesus, born among the Jewish people, was given a Jewish name *Jesus.* The name *Jesus* divinely given from heaven is the Greek translation of the Hebrew name *Yeshua* which also means *Joshua.* The original Gospel was written in Greek and that is why we come across the translated name Jesus. The name *Joshua* or *Jesus* as revealed in the Scriptures means *the Lord is salvation.* It is just as Moses was chosen to lead the people out of the wilderness and into the Promised Land, the same was Jesus to lead His People out of sin and into the presence of God. Jesus is also called *Christ* which is the English translation of the Greek word *Christos* which has the same meaning as the word *Messiah* or *The Anointed One.* In the Old Testament prophecies, the Messiah was promised to the children of Israel and Jesus fulfilled those prophecies. Jesus Christ, the Messiah was the phrase that expressed His complete identification with all humanity. Therefore, Jesus and Christ, is a two–fold designation combining the personal name Jesus and the title Christ, meaning *Anointed One* or *Messiah.* The title *Christ,* however, is quite significant in human history. This is because it is by this name coded *Jesus Christ* that every knee shall bow, and every tongue confess that He is Lord to the glory of God the Father.

Therefore, when we say *Jesus Christ,* first we are talking about the *Christ* or the *Messiah,* the *Righteous Lord.* Christ however signifies the divinity of Jesus. Therefore, the humanity of Christ is *Jesus* just as the divine part of Jesus, which is godly, is *Christ.* This means that Jesus Christ is fully man and fully God. Jesus Christ, being God and man is therefore able to take humanity and all of creation along in its path to the cross. The Bible talks about Christ in his human nature, that He is the visible discovery of the invisible God. He was begotten before any creature was made, which is the Scriptural way of representing eternity, and by which the eternity of God is represented to us (Colossians 1:15-23 NKJV). The universe exists because of Christ and it as for the idea that the universe was born in Him. The Scripture says, "For in Him were all things created" (Colossians 1:16-17 NKJV). This means Christ created all things collectively within the universe. It also means that, for Christ creation was an historical event. The creations of Christ include all the dimensions of the universe. That means Jesus Christ was before all things in time. Therefore, before anything was ever created, Jesus Christ was already there. That also means that before the beginning of time and before the universe ever existed, Jesus Christ was there. Jesus Christ is eternal God.

The part Jesus Christ had in creating the world and man goes beyond the Old Testament account of creation. The Apostle John opens his Gospel with the statement, "In the beginning was the Word, and the Word was with God, and the Word was God. The same was in the beginning with God. All things were made by Him; and without Him was not anything made that was made" (John 1:1-3 KJV). Now look carefully at the statement, "*in the beginning was the word.*" Which beginning? Many people identify this beginning to mean the same beginning mentioned in Genesis 1:1 (NKJV). But in truth, the revelation of John concerning the *Word* goes far beyond explanation. The *Word* which John was talking about is a *timeless Word* and it simply points to existence before the present time without referring to any point of origin. You may push back the *beginning* as far as you can, but according to John, the *Word* still is. Hence, the *Word* John is referring to is *eternal and timeless.* The *Word* therefore is not a creation that came into existence at *the beginning;* for before there was any beginning, there was already the *Word.* What John means in fact is that: From all eternity the Word existed. John intensely presents the truth, which is the basis of all truth, that Jesus Christ is the Son of God, and is God. John did not stop here. In the next phrase, he says, *"And the Word was with God and the Word was God".* Here we see one more time the verb *was,* pointing to the timelessness of the Word, meaning the *Word* was in company with God. This explains interaction and fellowship, which is an eternal one of course. John asserts that the *Word* and *God* are distinguishable and are not interchangeable. In fact, John was a Jew and as a Jew, he believed in *One Being* rightly called God. John is affirming the full Deity of Jesus Christ and informing us *God* and the *Word* have eternally co-existed.

The pre-existence of the historical Jesus Christ is proved throughout the Bible indicating that He created the world. The Bible declares that "All things were made by him; and without him was not anything made that was made" (John 1:3 KJV). *All things* mean every single detail of creation whether material or spiritual, angelic or human has come into being by Christ. This means all things came into existence by means of the pre-existent Word, and of all the things that now exist, none came into being apart from Him. Another translation says: Through him all things were made; without him nothing was made that has been made (John 1:3 NIV). This is one of the reasons why He is called *the image of God,* and the *first-born.* That means among the Godhead, He was the active Agent and creation was His function and work. The world is God's world and Christ made it, every element of it, one by one and systematically, He made them all. The Bible continues concerning Him: "He was in the world, and the world was made by Him, and the world knew Him not", (John 1:10 KJV). Christ who has made the world was tragically rejected by the world. He came to the world that was supposed to be His home, something that He Himself had created, and His own people in the world rejected Him. Furthermore, John now explains, "the Word became flesh, and dwelt among us, and we saw His glory, glory as of the only begotten from the Father, full of grace and truth" (John 1:14 NKJV). Once again, John through revelation explains that, when the *Word of God* became flesh, it was not the beginning of the existence of the Word. Rather, before the Universe existed there was the *Word.* The *Word* becoming flesh refers to a specific point of time known as the incarnation. That means the Son of God was actually made flesh. He came to the earth in the person of Jesus Christ. John used the word *Theo,* the very word that is consistently used for the Father just like in John 17:3 (NKJV), the *only true God* or as used in John 1 (NKJV) and Genesis 1-3 (NKJV). The term *the only true God* is used three times of Jesus in the Gospel and that include John 1:18 (NKJV) and in John 20:28 (NKJV). As mentioned earlier, the tradition of Judaism in which John was brought up does not permit the worship of many Gods. Therefore, it is true of what John perceives of Jesus Christ, that He is God. The *Word* is also the same *Word* Paul uses to describe man's nature with all its weakness and tendency to sin. This is a staggering revelation. Jesus Christ is God – fully God yet is man – fully man.

Muslims and Jews will not be comfortable with this revelation, that *The Word is God* and that both the *Word* and *God* refers to Jesus Christ. In the next chapter, detailed explanation is given to the reader why Jesus is *fully God*. This has been supported with a testimony of how the teacher and Imam of Martin (*not his real name*) who was then a Muslim, could not explain what the Quran says about the *Word*, or what distinguishes between Creator and Creation. The *Word* is the Greek word, which is the *Logos,* and it is a title of the Lord Jesus Christ and a personal name of Christ. The *Word* is used about twenty times in the New Testament. There is no room to speculate that God becoming a man was just a vision of someone's imagination. John is saying that he and others actually saw the *Word* become *flesh*. That means that Jesus Christ was beyond question God Himself who became man and partook of the very same flesh as all other men (1 John 1:1-4 NKJV). When John mentions that *The Word was with God,* it means the revelation of God, *the logos which was with God and was God* became a man. Simply, it means the *Logos* was Jesus Christ, God incarnated in the Flesh. It also means the *logos* and *Jesus Christ* are the same. It is in this connection that John explains, "No one has seen God at any time. The only begotten Son, who is in the bosom of the Father, He has declared Him" (John 1:18). The statement *"No man has seen God at any time,"* means our knowledge of God did not come from any man and the word *"declared"* means Jesus who is the *"Word"* has revealed to the world God the Father, and that is because it is only Jesus who knows all things about God the Father. This is exactly what He did also in the Old Testament. Jesus claimed He alone has seen God and that was because He was the one and the only Son of God (John 3:16 NKJV). He also claimed that He had come from God and that He had had the most intimate and deepest and honorable relationship with God (John 1:18 NKJV) and again that He had come to reveal and to proclaim the Father to the world (John 14:6; Rev. 14:7 NKJV).

John further explains the equality of Jesus Christ and God, "*I and my Father are one*" (John 10:30 NKJV). In His Oneness with God, Jesus qualifies for all the functions of a Savior and Lord. He qualifies as our High Priest. In His high priestly prayer, Jesus said to God: "I have glorified thee on the earth: I have finished the work which thou gavest me to do. Now, O Father, glorify thou me with thine own self with the glory, which I had with thee before the world, was made (John 17:4, 5 KJV). The reader may look at the statement the second time: "I have finished the work which you gave me to do", "Glorify me with your own self with the glory which I had with you before the world was made". This does not mean Jesus has no power of His own and that He could not do anything without God. Far from that, for Jesus has always given credit to God when it comes to making a choice or decision on earth. As a man, He always surrendered and was submissive to the Father, something He wants us to do and emulate, and even though He is God He walked in obedience to fulfil His Father's bidding. He is therefore the most important person in the history of the world.

In conclusion, it is laudable that such a person exists in history, and even though it might be difficult to exhaust all the truth about Him, history again makes Him comparable to none. It is also baffling to other religious men and women more when Christians say Jesus is the first born of all creation. It is intriguing to examine what it really means for God to be the first born of all His creations. It will therefore be interesting to open a new chapter about this topic of Jesus's humanity.

8. Jesus, the First Born of all Creations

It sounds quite controversial for non-Christians to hear Christians calling Jesus the Son of God and that is because Muslims have debated and disputed against every truth that underlies the fact that the Bible names Jesus as the first born of all creation. The word *firstborn* that the Bible uses literally refers to birth order which places the first-born child in the front roll (Colossians 1:15-18 NKJV). The impact that this truth makes concerning Jesus Christ has great significance to man. First, there emerged false teachings from the church in Colossian that attacked the divinity of Jesus Christ. There were in the church Gnostics that said Jesus was not the only mediator between God and man and that there were many ways or gods by which man could reach God. They also advocated that through knowledge and certain key words and learning, a person can have personal improvement and self-effort to gain acceptance with God. The Gnostics' way of serving God was like that of the Muslims who believe that it is good works that can earn a person favor before God. Whilst there is a natural way for a person to gain insight about God and religion, there is also the striking point that knowing about God as advocated by the Muslims and Gnosticism does not really make a person know God in person. This is because the truth in Jesus Christ goes beyond the thought and knowledge of man. God does not save a person because he thinks about God or knows something about religion. God does save a person through Jesus Christ. Jesus reveals that God saves a person who comes to God through Him and it is Him alone who redeems and forgives us our sins (Colossains1:14 NKJV). This is because Jesus Christ is the *first born* of all creation, the exact representation and manifestation of the very Person of God Himself. This leads to the fact that no particular type of lifestyle or knowledge or good works can bring us to God. The thoughts of the Gnostics or men were therefore not the thought of God. Their thought about Jesus being the first born of all creation was of the flesh. Just like the Muslims, they interpreted this to mean that just like Adam; Jesus Christ was the first created being of the universe.

The concept of the *first born of all creation* is a concept of great significance in the Old Testament. According to the tradition of the Jews, the firstborn son inherited his father's place as head of the family and receives the father's blessing and a double portion of the inheritance of the family (Deuteronomy 21:17 NKJV). This social tradition appears in several places in the New Testament where Jesus Christ is referred to as the firstborn. What does this mean? Was it because Mary gave birth to Him first before other children of Joseph or does this carry deeper theological connotations? There is also the title "firstborn of the dead" (Colossian 1:18 NKJV), which makes this discussion about Jesus of great theological importance, especially with Easter in the background. We are all children of God but in the case of Jesus, there is more to that than what the ordinary mind can feature out. We get a historical view about this after the Passover in Egypt. In Egypt God told the Israelites that every firstborn child would be set aside as His own (Exodus 13:2 NKJV), and the nation of Israel as a whole was generally referred to as God's "firstborn son" (Exodus 4:22 NKJV). This concept and practice therefore gives special status to the firstborn as the preeminent son and heir. King David is the most exalted of the kings of the earth, but the Bible calls him the Lord's first born (Psalm 89:27 NKJV), even though he was the youngest son of Jesse (1 Samuel 16:10–13 NKJV). The psalmist celebrates the kingship of David and his line with phrases like *the firstborn, the highest of the kings of the earth,* and the idea that the

Messiah's throne will be a *faithful witness*. Even though Manasseh was the first born of Joseph, it was Ephraim that was referred to as the Lord's first born (Jer.31:9 NKJV). These were first born in the sense of pre-eminence. John draws words and imagery from the Psalms of David in referring to Jesus as the firstborn of the dead (Psalms 89:1 NKJV).

In the New Testament, Jesus is shown to be the *new Israel,* as He becomes the culmination and fulfillment of God's promise to bless all the nations through Abraham (Galatians 3:7 NKJV). Abraham was used in this example to show that we can only be justified by faith. Abraham was the founder of the Jewish nation and was the person God used as a witness to other nations concerning the only true God (Gen. 13:14-17; 15:1-7; 35:9-12 NKJV). It was not Abraham keeping of the law that made God to justify him as righteous, but it was his faith in God. There was no law during the time of Abraham, but Abraham was justified as righteous when he believed what God had said, that He would give him a new nation, with a new people (Gal.3:8; Hebrew 11:9-19 NKJV). God made a promise to Abraham and in that promise, only one condition was attached to it, and Abraham had to believe. There was no works that was attached to this promise, but it was his faith that preceded his obedience. Therefore, as the scripture says, it is those who have believed God and His Word that are the children of God. It is in accordance with this that the scripture announced the Gospel to Abraham. That means God promised Abraham that he would be a great nation. In this promise was the seed of Abraham, which was Isaac, but the real promised seed was to come, and the Jewish nation was the nation through which the promised seed of God was to be born (Hebrews 11:9-19 NKJV). The promise of God in the seed of Abraham was therefore directed to a single person and that person is Jesus Christ. Jesus Christ therefore is the fulfillment of the promise to Abraham. God said to Abraham: *through you all the nations of the earth would be blessed*. The new nations apart from the nation of Israel constitute the nation of believers of Jesus Christ that God is creating to inherit the new heavens and earth ((Eph. 1:9-10; 2:11-18; 3:6; 4:17-19; Gal.3:16

NKJV). Here our mind is brought to the new Israel, which Jesus represents. For since it is through Israel that the righteous and true God would be known, the same shall the Son of God, the first born of all creation who is the true promised seed be born among the Jewish people. The culmination and fulfillment of God's promise to bless all the nations of the world therefore lie in stems from Jesus Christ, who is a type of Isaac according to the scriptures (Gen.15:2-3; 18:11; 22:10-13; Rom.4:18-22; Heb.11:19 NKJV). Jesus therefore fulfils the intended role of Israel as God's faithful firstborn son in His perfect life and sacrificial death, and God vindicates Him in His glorious resurrection. Paul calls Jesus Christ the *"firstborn over all creation"* in his letter to the Colossians (Col. 1:15 NKJV). Paul distinguishes between the divine nature of Christ and the earthly man Jesus, that those who believe in Jesus Christ would be conformed to His image. Jesus on the other hand shall have many brothers, among whom He is to be honored as the first and most preeminent person (Romans 8:29 NKJV).

The idea of Jesus being the *first born* is interpreted differently by both Muslims and the Jehovah Witness. The Jehovah Witnesses interpret the word *firstborn* to mean, *first created*. Jehovah Witness believe that Jesus is a created being. The Bible says the *"Word became flesh"* which does not necessarily mean it is a created thing (John 1:1, 14 NKJV); neither does it mean He is the first born in creation. What it means is that Jesus is the Lord over all creation, the first to be given preeminent position among men. The Muslims believe Jesus is created just like Adam, but He was not. Rather He was *the Word* that has been with God before any beginning. When we talk of the first born of all creation, it means Jesus is put before all things and it is in Him all things hold together (Col. 1: 17 NKJV). How can Christ be both the eternal Creator of all things and yet Himself be the firstborn? This implies that calling Jesus the first-born portrays Him as the heir of David, exalted and lifted up as the representative of His people. The Bible describes Him as *the head of the body*, which is the church. He is as well the beginning, the firstborn from among the dead so that He himself may become first in all things (Colossians 1:18

NKJV). *Beginning* means creative power. Before something is created, it is brought into being by someone who is greater. Jesus Christ was the Person who gave birth to the church. It is the idea of His mind and the result of His love that brought the church into existence, that the church will accomplish His purpose on earth. Therefore, He is the Person who is to be honored as the founder of the church. The scripture says, *in everything Jesus might have the supremacy.* That means in everything that God has ordained in the universe, Jesus is the first and the last. He was the first to rise from the dead and never to die again. In that sense there is a connection between the church of Jesus Christ and the resurrection. It is because of the resurrection that the church exists. There would be no church had Jesus not risen from the dead. Since Jesus was the first to rise from the dead, He stands as the pattern, the forerunner, and the perfect man to conquer death. If a person believes that Jesus died and resurrected, God takes that person's faith and counts the person as belonging to Christ. If the person dies, because he belongs to Christ, the Holy Spirit takes that person and transfers him right into the presence of God. Therefore, it is those who believe in the resurrection that makes the church of Jesus Christ. This is the true message and hope of the Gospel. Jesus Christ conquered death for the church, because it is the church that have trusted and believed in the resurrection, and for that reason when Christians die, the resurrection power of Jesus Christ transfers them into the eternal presence of God. Apart from the resurrection of Jesus Christ, there is no hope for humanity and without it; there would have been no hope for the church.

Further, to explain more regarding the term *"beginning"*, the Scripture indicates that Jesus is the firstborn from among the dead, which gives Him the foremost position of Lordship over all creation. Paul continues: *"so that He might become preeminent in all things."* So while Jesus is certainly the first to rise from the dead, the truth is hereby established that Jesus Christ is the sovereign Lord over all those who will likewise rise from the dead and He is preeminent in the things that concern the end or the ultimate of all things in the world. Jesus finally confirms His own word by saying "I am He who lives, and was dead, and behold, I am alive forevermore. Amen. And I have the keys of Hades and of Death" (Revelation 1:18 NKJV). This is a great assurance given to us by Jesus Christ through the Apostle John. When John saw Jesus, he was terribly afraid and fell at His feet as though he was dead. Jesus reached out with His hand and tenderly touched John assuring him He would not harm him. Jesus said to John "do not be afraid, I am the first and the last, the beginning and the end" (Rev.1:17 NKJV). John needed not to be afraid, because he was with the eternal Lord of the universe and the Savior of the world. This shows that Jesus is alive and dwells in the most awesome glory and lives forever and ever and because of the love He has for humanity, He makes it possible for us to be acceptable to God.

As the first born of all things, it was neither mighty deeds nor self-attestation that revealed the deeper secret of the nature of Jesus. The revelation about Him came through His life, His person, and what those closed to Him felt happened to them in His presence. Those who were closed to Him the time He was on earth knew that He was a man, just as human as any one of them. However, a change began to occur in their lives that only God could bring about. They knew their sins had been forgiven, a thing only God could do; they felt a love and compassion far beyond any man's capacity; they began to feel new life stirring in their hearts that only God could bring. The disciples lived with Him day by day. They ate with Him, they walked with Him, they slept with Him, they saw Him weep, and they watched Him pray. Surely, He was man through and through and yet there was something special and unique about Him, and no human being had ever demonstrated that uniqueness, except Him. The Scripture says, He is the eternal Creator who spoke the world into existence. In John He is called *"God"* (John 1:1 NKJV), and in Hebrews He is said to be the One who "laid the foundations of the earth" (1:10 NKJV). The book of Hebrews calls Him the "image of the invisible God" (Hebrews 1:3 NKJV). *Image* here means likeness or copy and expresses His deity. This involves more than just a resemblance or more than just a representation. It means He is God. In the book of Revelation, Jesus Christ refers to Himself as "the

Alpha and the Omega, the First and the Last, the Beginning and the End" (Rev. 22:13 NKJV). Indeed, the whole of Scripture teaches that Jesus Christ could be nothing other than the preexistent sovereign of the universe. As the first born of all creation, Jesus is also called the Son of Man. This is a topic worth discussing for the enlightenment of all people, especially Jews and Muslims.

9. Jesus the Son of Man

As first-born of all creation, Jesus almost invariably calls Himself in the New Testament *the Son of man*. He applies this name to Himself over eighty times so commonly as to be almost overlooked. Here are some examples; "For even the Son of Man did not come to be served, but to serve, and to give His life a ransom for many" (Mark 10:45 NKJV). "Foxes have holes and birds of the air have nests, but the Son of Man has nowhere to lay His head" (Mathew 8:20 NKJV). "The Son of man came eating and drinking" (Mathew 11:19 NKJV). "You know that after two days is the Passover, and the Son of Man will be delivered up to be crucified" (Mathew 26:2 NKJV).

Centuries ago, in the scriptures, the phrase *"Son of man"* (without the article *the*) was used frequently in the book of Ezekiel as a title of address by God to the prophet "Son of man, stand upon your feet" (Ezekiel 2:1 NKJV), "Son of man, I am sending you to the children of Israel" (Ezekiel 2:1-3 NKJV) and thereafter some ninety times in the book. The phrase in Ezekiel is a way of expressing the prophet's humanity and His identification with other people. Other familiar passages such as "What is man that thou art mindful of him, and the son of man that thou dost care for him" (Psalm 8:4 KJV)? This shows that the phrase is another way of saying *man*. This backward glance at the Old Testament makes it clear why the disciples probably never gave a second thought to Jesus calling Himself *the Son of man*. For, unmistakably, there was never in their minds any question of

His complete humanity. They were all sons of men; as the Muslims will say. Most of the times, Jesus hid His identity from the public. In this example, Jesus is the Son of Man, but not just an ordinary son of man, for it was only among His disciples that His identity is known as "the Christ, the Son of the living God" (Mathew 16:16 NKJV). Yet surely, it is of great significance; for it *the title Son of Man* says something about the humanity of Jesus that can be said of no other man. It means that Jesus was the full man and completely full God in a human form. The prophet Daniel sees one like *the son of man* coming to the ancient of Days to receive all power and dominion at the end of time (Daniel 7). Jesus claims that He is the Son of man, the Son of God incarnate in human flesh as the perfect man. As Son of man and the Last Adam, Jesus would overcome the four empires of the ancient world and would be enthroned at His Father's right hand. Jesus' ascension and enthronement at God's right hand, establishes not only His reign but also the dominion of His people. Jesus said, "They will see the Son of man coming" (Luke 21:27 NKJV). That means all men would see His return to the earth and everyone will acknowledge Him as Lord.

Jesus further identifies Himself as the Son of Man who sits enthroned at God's right hand as King of creation who determines the eternal destiny of every individual. It is important to note that the rule of this *"son of man"* also involves the rule of the *"saints"* (Daniel 7:18, 22 NKJV). It is worth noting that the sovereignty, power and greatness of all the kingdoms under heaven will be given to the saints of God Most High (Daniel 7:27 NKJV). The Kingdom of Jesus Christ, the King of Kings, will last forever and all rulers will serve and obey Him. The situation that results when dominion is given to the saints is called *His kingdom.* That means that Jesus, the Son of Man is the One to shows us the wonders and beauty of what it is to be truly human and gives us the perfect pattern to follow. Jesus, the Son of man is to show us how we should live with each other and how each one of us might be a son of man living like Him to the glory of God and the service of all others.

Jesus consistently referred to Himself as *the Son of man* and not as *the Son of God*. The reason is to recognize Jesus as *the Son of man* is of great significance for what is yet to be said about Him. For it is against this background that He raises the all-important question to the disciples: "But who do you say that I am?" (Mark 8:29 NKJV) The disciples have already replied to His first question, "Who do people say the Son of man is?" (Mathew 16:13 NIV); that some say John the Baptist; others say Elijah, and others Jeremiah or one of the prophets. In other words, Jesus was unquestionably a prophet as the Muslims claim; and among the greatest if not the greatest in the eyes of the people. He was indeed a human being, and a prophet who by definition is a representative for God, according to the people. Therefore, by that very question two things are taken into consideration: first, the answer others are giving is not adequate; secondly, it is highly important that they speak for themselves by answering the question: *"Who do people say that the Son of Man is?* Jesus wanted to know the mind of His disciples concerning Him, for He called Himself *the Son of Man* instead of declaring to His disciples that He is *the Son of God*. They have never thought of who the Son of man is, but they knew who their master is. Some thought Jesus was John the Baptist, who had been executed by King Herod, returned from the dead. Some said He was Elijah or Jeremiah or one of the ancient prophets. Jesus asked them *"what do you think I am"?* Instantly Simon Peter replies for the disciples, "You are the Christ, the Son of the living God" (Matthew 16:16 NKJV). Jesus had asked this question the second time and that sounded critical, for the question was asked much more emphatically *"But you, who do you say that I am?* The answer given by Peter is unmistakable and was given from personal conviction, because it shows Peter's personal trust in Jesus Christ. Perhaps Peter did not understand fully all that was involved in Jesus Christ being the Son of God or the Son of man. Peter did not really understand Jesus's true mission (Mathew 16:21–23) and was lapsed into believing that Jesus was a physical descendant of David come to lead the Jewish nation to independence and glory. That was why the disciples were shocked and disappointed of His unexpected death. Nevertheless, Peter's confession was simple and from his heart, for it was a matter of trust and conviction, that Jesus Christ is the Son of God. God has been waiting for this declaration to be made when He personally put this in the heart of Peter. How did Jesus respond to Peter? "Blessed are you, Simon son of Jonah, for this was not revealed to you by man, but by my Father in heaven" (Mathew 16:17 NIV). Jesus was not after the confession of Peter about Him being the Christ. Rather, He was after the confession that confirms His deity as the Son of the living God and the fact that the disciples trust in the saving grace, which He was sent for the sake of the world.

Though Jesus is the *Son of Man* and among the mighty prophets, He is much, much more than that. He is also the Messiah and as prophesied by the Prophets, *the Messiah is the Son of God*. We see an interesting observation regarding Peter's respond concerning *"the Son of Man"* as *"the Christ"*. The fact is many people hoped for a Messiah, but they never went beyond thinking of a Son of man of the line of David, who would restore His people to power and prosperity. They never thought of Him also as the Son of God. Indeed, they were so occupied with the Old Testament teaching which says "Hear, O Israel: The Lord our God is one Lord" (Deuteronomy 6:4 NKJV); that to consider the *Son of man* was also *the Son of God* and the *Messiah*, was hardly conceivable. Yet we find here Simon Peter, who is pre-informed from the Old Testament teachings, testifying, "You are the Christ, the Son of the living God" (Mathew 16:16 NKJV). To further affirm Peter's confirmation, Jesus does not rebuke Peter as if he were indulging in fantasy. Rather Jesus replies him: "Blessed are you, Simon Bar-Jonah! Flesh and blood have not revealed this to you, but my Father who is in heaven" (Mathew 16:17 NKJV). No rebuke at this time, but to separate the sheep from the wolf, Jesus did rebuke Peter later when he wanted to restrain Him from going to the cross. You can know when truth about Jesus is being enforced for the sake of evidence. The testimony about Jesus from Peter was therefore the truth.

Jesus Christ is *the Son of man* and continues so to be as the rest of the narrative unfolds but at the same time, He accepts the testimony that He is *the Son of God.* Jesus answered Peter with what only comes by revelation that; *"flesh and blood has not revealed this to you, but my Father."* With all His love and diligence, Jesus fulfilled that commission for which His Heavenly Father had given Him, directing everything toward His Father's glory. As the Son of man and a man Himself, He felt pity for all people especially for the poor and the underprivileged. He wished everyone well and was willing to bear anything in order to ease their suffering. He bore all conceivable affronts and insults from the ungrateful crowd with the greatest meekness and did not vent His anger on those who slandered Him and plotted intrigues against Him. Some who bore Christ ill-will called Him a sinner and lawbreaker; others called Him a carpenter's son and a shallow person whilst others said He was a friend of drunkards and sinners. On several occasions, Christ's enemies attempted to stone Him or toss Him from the hill. The Jewish scribes called His divine teachings deceitful; and when He healed the sick, raised the dead, or exorcised demons, they explained away these miracles as the deeds of an evil spirit. Some even openly called Him possessed. The Lord Jesus, being Almighty God, could have destroyed them all with one word. Instead, He pitied them as spiritually blind and prayed for their welfare and for their salvation. That is what Christians are supposed to do, to imitate their Master. Unfortunately, many people have mistaken such an attitude from Christians to be weakness and for that matter have taken them for granted. Many Christians have undergone suffering trying to imitate Christ and have suffered severe persecution for their faith.

Even though Jesus being the Son of man identified Himself as God, He never went about broadcasting that He was God. He tried as much as possible to hide His identity only to show humility as a man who had come to the world to suffer for our sake. It is in this significant attitude of Jesus that none could be measured up to Him. For example, the blind man who is also a beggar by name Bartimaeus has heard about Jesus and believes in Him that He could heal him of his blindness and set him free. He then cries out to Jesus: *"Jesus, Son of David, have mercy on me!"* (Luke 18:38 NKJV). Jesus to whom this title had never been attributed, heard the cry of the desperate blind man and did not turn His back on him. Turning to him, Jesus called him to come forward to ask whatever he wanted. All that he wanted was to be healed. Jesus the most compassionate Lord granted his request, gave him back his sight and saved him.

This blind man had knowledge about whom Jesus was and acknowledged Him as *the Messiah* and *the Son of David,* which was the title used for the Messiah and validly applied to Jesus. Jesus, according to the scriptures was the Son of David predicted from the beginning and as we have explained, He was much, much more than that. Bartimaeus used what he had heard or understood concerning the Messiah and, in his desperation, did not beg for money or bread. All he desperately needed was to have his sight restored. He was rebuked but he never gave up. He persisted and cried out until he was given attention. Jesus passing by was his last hope and only chance to receive mercy. Perseverance is the key. For that is how God wants us to do; to be persistent in our Christian life, so that we can stand against every odd and eventuality until God gives us attention. The critical step the blind man took is what is preached in the Christian church today. It is important for a person to believe that Jesus Christ is the promised Messiah, the one true God sent to die for the sins of the world (Romans 10:13-17 NKJV). A person can only be saved if he or she believes that Jesus is his or her Lord and Personal Savior.

Turning to the Pharisees Jesus asked them: "What do you think of the Christ, whose son is He? They said to Him, 'The son of David'. He said to them, 'How is it then that David, inspired by the Holy Spirit, calls Him Lord, saying, "The Lord said to my Lord, sit at my right hand, till I put thy enemies under thy feet"? If David then calls Him Lord, how is He his son by calling Him "Lord" (Mathew 22:42-46 NKJV). This question posed to the Pharisees is a critical question to people who have not known Jesus Christ as the Son of God. Jesus asked this question because He wanted to stir them to think about the Messiah. He did not ask them what they thought of Him but indirectly what they think of the Messiah. This is because the destiny of a person is always determined by what he thinks about salvation and the Savior of the world. Jesus asked them to mention whose son is the Messiah and what was His origin. The Messiah was to be the person who is to execute perfect judgment and to rule and govern all lives. Where will He come from? Will He come from earthily parents or from God? Even though this question may be asked, this will not lead a person to the truth. Jesus asked them the most critical question, but they could not come out to the truth. The Pharisees answered Jesus by giving the thought of man, that the Messiah is the son of David, a man. They said we know the title of the Messiah, which was *"the Son of David"*. This is the confirmation from the Old Testament, that the Messiah was to set the people of Israel free and that He would be a human being. There was this important idea about the Messiah that *He was to be of a divine origin of God Himself.* This was not acceptable to the people of Israel. This was because as humans, they have always thought of the Messiah as a deliverer in terms of power and fame, that he will wield much political and military power.

Nevertheless, Jesus pointed out to the Pharisees and the people of Israel that the Messiah is Lord, the Lord of David (Mathew 22:43-45 NKJV). The Bible pointed out that David called the Messiah Lord, speaking by the Spirit; that David's words were said under the inspiration of the Holy Spirit. Jesus confirms that whilst it is true that the Messiah comes from the line of David, His power and royal dignity is far greater than that of David's, for David addresses Him as "my Lord" (Psalm 110:1 NKJV), and when it comes to exercising rule as King, it is only Yahweh (Psalm 110:2 NKJV). So we see David making a distinction between God and the Mediator and promising the Mediator majesty and power and authority which is only for a person who is everlasting and who will forever be God (Eph. 1:20-23, Hebrews 2:9; Phil.2:5-11 and Revelation 5:1-10; 12:5 NKJV). On the other hand, the same Lord that is exalted is the son of David (Psalm 132:17, 2 Samuel 7:12-13 NKJV), signifying that Christ is both man and God. For David calling Him son means that He is the descendant and offspring of David (Rev. 22:16; Isaiah 11:1, 10 NKJV).

Jesus was therefore telling the Jews that man's concept of the

Messiah, as being only human is inadequate and totally misunderstood. They have only put their minds on earthly power, of military and national affairs. Just like we see in the world today, there is no way a mere man can bring about perfect deliverance or freedom to the world. The Messiah is the only man that has no limitations and that is because He is also Lord and God from Heaven. Jesus, the true Messiah of man was at this point claiming to be the Son of God, and He tried to teach them by saying that man's concept concerning the Messiah has to go beyond human power and ability. It was therefore important for man to seek God with all his heart in order to have total deliverance and freedom, which are impossible for man to deliver completely. Because of the love of God for man, God sent His Son to the earth, offered Him as sacrifice in order that all might receive salvation and eternal life. Salvation was therefore the key factor for Jesus, the Son of Man for coming to the world. That was what was inscribed in the original plan in the blueprint of God that God was to bring us back to the great perfect plan He had always had for us. By so doing God manifested Himself in the flesh, being called both *the Son of Man* and *the Son of God*. As the incarnated Word of God, Jesus came as the perfect man to dwell among us.

10. Jesus Christ, the Son of God

The evidence as declared from the above chapter testifies that Jesus Christ is man by nature and He is also the first born of all creation, which gives Him the foremost position of Lordship over all creation. In this chapter, we will go a little bit deep to explain the mysteries behind God`s Son and help Muslims and Jews and also atheist to understand what Christians means when they say *Jesus is the Son of God*.

Of all the religious figures throughout history, and throughout the world, Jesus has been branded as unique for many reasons. Some of the reasons include the fact that His birth was foretold by Prophets like Isaiah and Micah. This birth was a miraculous birth. The most important arguments that have raised contention is Jesus being classified as *God and the only the Son of God*. Many Muslims and Jews believe that Jesus' claim of being the Son of God has no sufficient proof enough, and that there is not enough evidence that He is God. They highlight the fact that there is a clear distinction between the expressions *God the Son* and *Son of God,* and that the former implies deity whereas the latter does not. They further contend that Jesus never called Himself *God the Son*, but used a title, which is often applied to others without implying that these other persons are divine beings. It is rather unfortunate that most Muslims find offensive the very belief that is central to the Christian faith; the assertion that Jesus Christ is the *Son of God*.

Why should Christians just assume that Jesus necessarily claimed to be God because He said He was God's Son and they have no evidence to justify that? One very important factor to take into consideration is that Christians do have some important common ground with Muslims when it comes to the person of Jesus. Among others, the Quran teaches that Jesus was born of a virgin (Sura 19:20) and that He is a Prophet (Sura 2:136). The Quran also teaches that Jesus is among those closest to God (Sura 3:45) and that He taught a message of kindness and compassion (Sura 57:27). The Quran again teaches that Jesus healed the sick and raised the dead by the power of God (3:49); that He miraculously fed the hungry (Sura 5:112.); and that He is alive now in heaven (3:55); and that He will return at the end of the age (43:61). Remarkably enough, and unknown to Muslims, the Quran affirms that *"Jesus is the Messiah and the Word of God"* (3:45 and 4:171). The evidence that Jesus is the Word of God as stated in the Quran is something Muslims have decided not to understand. These assertions are all evidences proved in the Bible. More mysterious is why Muslims claim they honor Jesus but ascribe much more honor to Prophet Mohammed than they do to Jesus, even though they know Jesus is more divine than Mohammed. In principle, many Muslims will not say the name of Jesus without adding *"Peace be upon Him"*, which in Arabic implies that they hail Him with respect. Why Muslims will not accept Jesus as God and God's Son as proved by the Quran is difficult to understand.

In order to raise more doubt surrounding the Sonship of Jesus to God, Muslims scholars have met Christians in the arena of debates to spell out their reasons why they believe Jesus is not the Son of God. In one of the debates of Sheik Joe (not his real name) versus his Christian counterpart on the divinity of Jesus, Sheik Joe stated that no Muslim is a proper Muslim if he does not believe in Jesus. It is difficult to understand what type of belief the Sheik was talking about since Muslims do not accept the most important beliefs of Christians; *that Jesus Christ is the Son of God and that He died and resurrected on the third day.*

The Quran says: *"God is unique, the source* (of everything). *He has not fathered anyone nor was He fathered, and there is nothing comparable to*

Him!" (Quran 112:1-4). The Quran continues: *"Such was Jesus, the son of Mary; it is a statement of truth, about which they vainly dispute. It is not befitting to the majesty of God, that He should beget a son. Glory be to Him! When He determines a matter, He only says to it, "Be" and it is"* (Quran 19:34-35). The reader can refer to the testimony of Martin (not his real name) in chapter eleven of this book. Martin explains the reason why God has no tongue but can talk, has no eyes but see, and therefore can have a Son without a wife. Besides, if Muslims believe in the Quran and what it says about Jesus then why do they fail to believe in His death and resurrection? Perhaps Muslims have a general perception that the one God of Abraham is not triune God and has not become incarnate among us. Though they believe the New Testament, the Torah, and the Psalms as God's inerrant Word, many still believe the Bible contains untrue story about Jesus. Some believe that people have so thoroughly altered the original text of the Bible that what we have today is not reliable. Some do argue that some of this alteration justifies the claim that the Bible never said that *Jesus is the Son of God.* Unfortunately, it is Jesus being named as *The Son of God* that Moslems find deeply offensive about the Christian religion. However, this is only a mere speculation with unfounded facts, simply because Muslims themselves have not searched nor understood what the Quran itself says about Jesus being *The Son of God.* Therefore, it is advisable that every true Moslem takes time to search and compare what the Quran and Bible say concerning this delicate subject. The conclusion is that both the Bible and the Quran testify that Jesus is truly *The Son of God.*

The perceptions of Muslims about the Bible and Jesus are not marginal issues. However, and more importantly, the issue of truth about the Christian faith is that, if you remove the Trinity, the Incarnation, and the Cross from the doctrine and teachings of the Christian faith, you have removed virtually all that Christians consider necessary to salvation. The Gospel is nothing more than the virgin birth, the atoning death and the resurrection of Jesus Christ. You cannot pull out these central substances from the Gospel, replace them with substitutes and still have a Gospel. It does not work that way. Why should Christians be very faithful to their call if the Muslim allegation is valid? This is because Christians see much better in the mirror than Muslims see when it comes to teachings in the Bible and faith in Jesus Christ, who is the Word of God incarnate. It may also be assumed that Muslims see better in the mirror of the Quran, but it is also a fact that most of the messages found in the Quran were borrowed from the Bible. When Christians use the phrase *The Son of God,* most Muslims hear something very different from what Christians believe and from what the Bible affirms. It is very important to look at the two sides, from both the Quran and from the Bible points of view in order to arrive at a sound conclusion about what it means to use the term *The Son of God.* On the other hand, if Muslims believe totally in the Quran and on that basis do what they do, it is not legitimate for them to look into the Bible to decide what is right and what wrong and what is not supposed to be there.

Moreover, if Muslims adhere to what is in the Quran as truth against what is in the Bible, were those truths not mere fittings put in the Quran purposely to prove that the Quran is the authentic and sacred word of God? For example, when we look at the Muslims' daily prayers, we realize that this involves reciting short passages from the Quran. One of the daily shorter passages Muslims recite in the Quran goes like this: *"He is God the One, God the Absolute Eternal, He does not beget, nor is he begotten, nor is there anything like unto Him."* These are written to remind devoted Muslims that God does not beget, nor is God begotten and to make a mockery of the truth concerning Jesus Christ that He cannot be the Son of God. More or less, Arabic which is basically the foundational language for the Quran uses the word for *beget* as *walada.* This word is almost as used in the book of Psalm "You are my son; today I have begotten you" *(Psalm 2:7 NKJV).* This is translated, as *"I have become your father".* The meaning provided in Arabic has a narrower definition and generally refers begetting through the sexual union of male and female which is carnality. This in principle is not what the Bible teaches about Jesus, and not what Christians believe. Bear in mind that the verb *walada* and the related noun *walad* which means son or child is clear in other passages that the Quran addresses whether God has children or not. The Quran asks, *"How could God have a son (walad) when He does not have a female consort?"* (Sura 6:101). Interestingly enough, when Arab Christians speak about Jesus Christ as the Son of God, they generally use a different Arabic word for Son, *Ibn,* which cognates to the Hebrew word *ben,* which has a broader range of meaning than *walad.* This is not to say that Arab Christians never use the verb *walada* in a metaphorical or no carnal sense. However, when Muslims use this word, they nearly always mean it in a literal, carnal sense. By contrast, the Quran frequently uses words in a metaphorical sense. Therefore, when Christians say, *"we believe Jesus is the Son of God,"* often what the Muslim hears is: *"we believe God had sexual relations with Mary and carnally produced an illegitimate divine-human offspring."* This is repugnant to both Muslims and Christians alike. This is one of the reasons why some Muslims are offended by the title *The Son of God.*

There are several other examples in the Bible that reject the idea of any sexual begetting (Psalm 45:6 NKJV). The Scripture says concerning Jesus: "But about the Son he says, "Your throne, O God, will last forever and ever, and righteousness will be the scepter of your kingdom" (Hebrew 1:8 NKJV). God said this about Christ and no other person. Here the Son is addressed as *God* by God the Father; that is God the Father calls Jesus Christ God. God the Father is saying that Jesus Christ has the same nature, being and character as He has. This gives an explicit meaning that Jesus Christ is Himself God and He is the One who sits in dignity and dominion with power over the entire universe. We see another example, which says that all human beings are in some sense *"God's offspring"* (Acts 17:28, 29 NKJV). Obviously, we see an example which referred to as *Son of God* and this reference has nothing to do with carnal begetting (Luke 3:38 NKJV). It is interesting to note that Jesus Christ was called the son of David and the genealogy goes on through to Adam until Jesus is mentioned as the Son of God. This was the common title and popular concept of the Messiah, who would under God conquer the world and promote God's majesty on earth. So that from His throne which is the throne of David, He would bring judgment upon the nations and peoples of the earth. Jesus was the Adamic heir and therefore was qualified to be the Messianic High Priest, the perfect High Priest who is the mediator between man and God. When Muslims say God has no son, they also mean most of them would not use the term *children of God* to refer to human beings in general. However, most Muslims agree that this term is not offensive. Quite often we hear Muslim leaders and scholars use the term *children of God* in reference to those who believe in the God of Abraham or to human beings in general. Similarly, most Muslims would not refer to God as our *Father* in this sense, but they do not necessarily find this offensive either. On a few occasions, some Muslim leaders and scholars affirm (with qualifications) that God is our Father in the sense of being a loving provider who cares for us, disciplines us, teaches us, and takes delight in us. When Muslims argue about the title *The Son of God Most High,* their conclusion is that just like Adam, we are all sons and children of God, therefore, Jesus cannot be the Son of God. In the English language when a definite article is used to describe a person, it is hardly to say this applies to anyone else. The angel did not say He should be called *Son of God Most High* like any son at all just like the Muslims say, *we are all children of God.* The angel said, He shall be called *The Son of God Most High.* It is true we are all sons and daughters of God, but there is not a single person in the scriptures, that is termed *the son of God* or for that matter *the Son of Man.* It is only Jesus Christ that has those tittles. We are sons and daughters of God in the sense of being His creatures. But for us to become sons and daughters of God in the salvational sense, children who have a living relationship with a loving and caring God, there should be a process that qualifies us to be called so.

There are several passages in the Bible that refer to those who believe in Jesus as *"children of God"* (John 1:12, 13 NKJV). John explains those who believe on His name are given the power or the right to become children of God. The word *to become* means to become something a person is not. That means that when a person receives Jesus Christ into his or her life as Lord and Savior, Jesus

Christ gives that person the power and the right to become something he or she is not; that is a child of God. Further, the Bible mentions the idea of sonship in God in Exodus where God told Moses to tell Pharaoh that Israel is His son (Exodus 4:22-23 NKJV). The place where the term *the sons of God* is used for the first time in the Bible is in Genesis 6:2 where fallen angels came to sleep with the daughters of men. Here the fallen angelic creatures were called the sons of God because they were not of human agents. Nevertheless, for us when a person is born again and has accepted Jesus Christ as His Lord and personal Savior, that person becomes a son or daughter of God and that is only by adoption. Therefore, through adoption a person can be called son of God. This is not the same for Jesus because Jesus is not an adopted son of God. So being a child of God and having the right to call God your father is something that only born-again Christians are entitled to (John 1:12-13 NKJV). Unfortunately for Muslims, since Allah is a distant God and cannot have a son (Sura 39:4), they cannot be children of Allah. For Christians, since Jesus is the Son of God in human flesh (John10:36-38 NKJV), it is only a life changing relationship that makes God deal with us not as enemies but that we are able to approach His throne with boldness (Hebrews 11:19 NKJV) and with the full assurance of faith (Hebrews 11:22 NKJV). Therefore, in the Christian faith being a child of God means adopted through faith in Jesus Christ who is the source of our hope and the security of our future (Ephesians 4:1 NKJV).

Though the Quran refers to Jesus as *God's Word,* most Muslims do not understand that term in the way Christians do. It is clear that the biblical term *Son* is not referring to literal, carnal begetting. It is describing a unique, eternal, spiritual relationship between Jesus and God. Muslims' objection here is not to the term *Son* itself, but to the idea that God was manifested in human flesh and that Jesus Christ is that true manifestation. On that note, Christians can have a more constructive conversation with Muslims if they think about the relationship of God's Word to God's own being. The Islamic theological tradition has a rich heritage of vigorous debate about the relationship of God's Word to God's Essence. The Quran, like the Bible, teaches that all things were created by *God's Word,* that is, by God's speaking to them and saying, *"Be!"* (Sura 16:40). The Bible affirms this by saying God spoke all things into being *"let there be",* and there was (Genesis 1:3 NKJV). The majority of the Sunni community conclude therefore that *God's Word* itself is eternal and uncreated. They also conclude that *God's Word"* is not identical with *God's Essence,* but it is anything other than God; rather *God's Word* is eternal and uncreated. Some Sunni theologians conclude further that since God's Word is manifest in the Holy Quran, therefore the Quran is both the eternal, uncreated quality of speech in God and the created, temporal expression of that eternal Word. That is what Christians are telling Muslims that the *Eternal Word* is God, the Second Person of the Trinity. Some important differences exist between this doctrine and the mainstream Christian understanding of the two natures of Christ. Here we have *divine* which is uncreated, and *human* which is created, and then that of the relationship of the divine Word, the Logos to the Father. We are not just supposed to overlook or ignore those differences. That is because there are enough similarities that can serve as bridge for understanding, so that when Christians explain what they believe, Muslims may understand accurately what Christian intend to say, whether they agree to it or not. The most important point here is that Muslims should not take the belief of Christians concerning the divinity of Jesus Christ for granted.

Many Christians can understand what a powerful emotional impact the term *the Son of God* has on many Muslims. This is because there are certain connotations that are connected to some words, despite the fact that these words assume new meanings or change of meaning in specific socio-linguistic contexts. This makes it quite difficult to separate *the Son of God* in the Bible from its true original meaning. Even Muslim with background in Christianity, who understand what *the Son of God* means and accept that meaning, sometimes struggle with using the phrase. The feelings they associate with the phrase *the Son of God* inevitably prompts them to think of the idea of illegitimate offspring of a sexual union between God and

Mary. Does the suggestion that Jesus is illegitimate offend Christians and Muslims alike? What about the notion that God had sexual intercourse with Mary? Of course, such a concept offends everyone. It should definitely offend anyone who believes in the status of Christ as Messiah of man and Creator of the universe. This is precisely how many Muslim feel even after Christian have tried to clarify what they understand about Jesus and what they do mean by the term *the Son of God* to them. The point however is, does it matter if Muslims' opinion regarding what the Bible says is not taken into consideration? It does not matter much since there is reliable evidence to the scriptures that Jesus is the Son of God. What matters most is that many Muslims may not live to have the real encounter with their Lord and Savior. Therefore, it is absolutely important for Muslims to identify with Christians to look at the truth of the content of the Bible starting from the Old Testament prophecy. Meaning that, since Muslims cannot dictate to Christians what they must change in the Bible and what should not; it is recommended they look critically into the meaning the Bible conveys with the phrase *the Son of God*. Muslims who have no proper understanding about how this phrase *the Son of God* is used, have to be careful to draw their conclusion. That is because the Quran in diverse ways mentions *the name of Jesus as the Son of God*, but Muslims have not come to the full understanding of what that means, let alone who Jesus Christ really is or what the term *the son of God* actually means to them.

The origin of the term *Son of God* as a messianic tittle comes when David wanted to build a temple for the Lord, but the Lord promised to raise up a descendant of David who would build an eternal temple whose throne God would established forever (2 Samuel 7; 1 Chronicles 17 and 22 NKJV). God says of this future messianic ruler: "I will be His father, and He will be my Son. I will never take away my love from Him" (1 Chronicles 17:13 NKJV). Here the title *Son of God* may not necessarily imply any divine status. However, our explanation as Christians is that, this does not in any sense imply carnal begetting. In other biblical passages, we come across *Son of God* or for that matter *children of God* which have other meanings. An interesting mode of dialogue between Muslims and Christians is that, most Muslims would not disagree with the term *Son of God* as used in the Bible. The concern however is, why do Muslims challenge the authenticity of the Bible when the historic evidence of the Bible does not derive from the Quran? If it does, then there should be no dispute whatsoever between the thoughts of Muslims and that of Christians.

In the real sense the phrase *the Son of God* has different meanings in different contexts in the Bible sense. The first sense, which most Bible scholars see as its most common meaning in the Gospels, is simply a messianic title which is more or less equivalent to Messiah, Son of David, or King of Israel (John 1:49; 11:27 NKJV). The Bible affirms all that took place in the life of Jesus on earth in accordance with what had been prophetically written about Him, which is to make us believe that Jesus is the Christ, the Son of God, and that by believing in His name we may have eternal life (John 20:31 NKJV). The claim of Jesus to be the Son of God is also confirmed when Jesus was brought before the High Priest. The Bible says the High Priest put Jesus under oath to answer, *"if He is the Son of God"*. The High Priest used his office as the representative of God and demanded an answer: ""I charge you under oath by the living God: Tell us if you are the Messiah, the Son of God" (Mathew 26:63–68 NIV), he asked Jesus. Jesus answered, *"Yes, it is as you say"* (Mathew 26:64 NLT). This was a strong confirmation! What happened after Jesus had said He was the Christ, the Son of God? The Bible says the High Priest tore his clothes. Why did he do that? He did that because according to the Jewish tradition, when they hear the name of God being dishonored or blasphemed, they tore their clothes; a sign which means the person has committed an abomination, an offence which carried the death penalty (2 Kings 18:37; 19; Isaiah 36:22;27:1; Acts 14:14 NKJV). Jesus Christ had thus committed blasphemy which was punishable by death among the Jewish people (Lev. 24:16; Acts 7:58 NKJV). If Jesus did not confirm that He is the Son of God, the High Priest would not have rented his cloths and said He had spoken blasphemy. What did they do to Him after He had said so? They spit on His face, buffeted Him and smote Him and finally killed Him.

The above facts are therefore important for our education; that when the Bible uses the term *Son of God,* it is making a critically important point that requires that a person pays attention to it. In the Gospel of John for example, the term is more-or-less equivalent to the *Word of God* who is God's self-expression and the visible manifestation of the invisible God. The Gospel of John says the *Word of God* was eternally with God and is *God,* and that through *God's Word* all things were created, and that this *Word* was manifested in *Jesus Christ,* and that we have seen His glory (John 1:1 NKJV). John adds: "No one has ever seen God, but the one and only Son, who is Himself God and is in closest relationship with the Father, has made Him known" (John 1:18 NKJV). God's Son, Jesus Christ, was made flesh and blood; He became a man and there is no greater message than this that God's Son became flesh. This is what John the Baptist bore witness to, that Jesus is superior to him. This simply explains that Jesus Christ is *God and only God,* who is at the Father's side and proves that God became flesh. John uses the term *Son* in this sense in several of his passages. Jesus however, made it clear that everyone should "honor the Son just as they honor the Father. And whoever does not honor the Son does not honor the Father, who sent him" (John 5:18–26 NKJV). Jesus therefore affirms that by talking about His relationship with God in this way, He was making Himself equal or identical with God. Jesus had already confirmed His oneness with God by saying, "'I and the Father are one" (John 10:30) NKJV, and "anyone who has seen me has seen the Father' (John 14:9 NKJV). He made this astounding claim to show that all authority belongs to Him (John 5:17-30 NKJV). How could He make such claim? Since He proclaimed that, it simply means He possessed equality with God. The Bible confirms the relationship that connects the *Word* and *Son* to God the Father in the light of the Bible's strong assertion that God is one. That the term *Son of God* means God; the Son thus is accredited in the teachings of the Trinity as the Second Person of the Trinity. Another outstanding claim Jesus made was calling

God "My Father" and not "our Father" (John 5:17-18 NKJV). In this example, Jesus was claiming a unique relationship, a Father-Son union with God and now note the fact that this was understood by the Jews that He said, *"God was His Father"* and that He was making Himself *"equal with God."*

The difference between Muslims and Christians concerning this revelation is due to a communication problem. Whilst there should be no concrete objection to Christian doctrine when it comes to the issue of the title *Son of God,* Muslims in principle reject the central idea of what Christians affirm to be an attested truth. This is due to the literal meaning of *Son of God* which communicates to Muslims something that is entirely different from what the Bible affirms. Some Muslims think it will be adequate to change the way we translate the New Testament phrase of *Son of God* and find an equivalent expression that will communicate more accurately what the Bible intends to deliver. The question however is, should we translate differently what is written in the Bible because of what Muslims believe or do not believe? Not at all! This is because the Bible being the true word of God, was written before the Quran came to existence. The Quran has already proved the Bible to be true, as it asks all Muslims to consult the Bible regarding all matters. It is based on this principle that one can defend the Bible, that it stands tall and holds every detail truth concerning Jesus being the Son of God. Christians do not need to search for higher, and more complex semantic connotations of the *Father* and *Son* relationship than what is found in the Bible. In addition, the term *the Son of God* is so central to the Christian theological tradition, that most Muslims are very much aware, that the phrase is supposed to be in the Bible. If Christians replace it with an equivalent or a variant term to suit Muslims, it means they are confirming the Muslims' allegation that the Bible has been altered. It would therefore confirm the contention of the enemies of the truth, that the credibility of the Bible has been undermined.

Whilst many Muslims are put under siege when it comes to believing the divinity of Jesus Christ, there are also many Christians who are ill informed about their own faith. When these Christians try to explain their faith to Muslims, they reluctantly express views the Church has historically understood as heretical. For example, the Quran asserts that Jesus was created like Adam from the dust (Quran 3:59). In response to that, some Christians assert that Jesus is in no sense a created human being. The Christian doctrine teaches that Jesus has two natures, which are *divine* and *human*, and that these are *united* in one person. His divine nature (*the Word/Logos*) is uncreated (John 1:1 NKJV). However, His human nature is like us in every way except in sin (Hebrews 2:17; 4:15 NKJV). That means Jesus was created from the dust and temporal just like us apart from the sinful nature, which makes Him very different from us as human beings. Jesus, therefore, being a man qualifies to become our great High Priest, and that was the reason why He was made like us, that He might be a merciful and faithful High Priest to us. He needed to do this in order to experience the conditions and trial we go through as humans.

There are other Christians also who explain to Muslims that Jesus' soul was divine and was clothed in a human body. The problem with this is that if Jesus did not have a fully human soul, then He was not like us in every way and tempted like us yet without sin. Other Christians, who are sensitive to the plight of Muslims, emphasize so strongly the separation between human and divine in Christ that they describe Jesus as nothing more than a human being indwelt by God. There are matured Christians deeply rooted in the word of God, who are the right vessels the Holy Spirit can use to teach Muslims and to bring them to understand the divine and human nature of the person of Jesus Christ. Lay Christians also need to avoid loopholes in their understanding of the Person of Christ in order to be able to help Muslims to know the real Jesus who is both man and God. Lay Christians should not forget that Jesus Christ in His divine nature is the Logos and is fully God and that in His full nature is human and that He is of the same essence as we are. These two natures of God are both united in one person, Jesus Christ and that the union of Jesus and Christ does not remove the distinction existing between the two natures. These two attributes of Jesus Christ are quite indispensable to our redemption.

At this juncture, what Jews, atheist, and Muslims need to understand is that, the salvation of humans depends on the person of Christ. As many Christian thinkers throughout the centuries have pointed out: If Christ were not God, He could not save us, because only God can save us. But if Christ were not human, He could not save us because only someone who is like us in every way except sin can represent us as our high priest offering Himself in atonement for our sins. The salvation of the human race therefore depends upon the fact that, Jesus Christ is both fully divine and fully human, and that these two natures are united but distinct in one person, that is, the Son of God. It is clear and without doubt, that Jesus Christ is revealed in the Scriptures as the Son, with His Father as God who is also the Head of the Trinity, and the Holy Spirit as the Spirit of God. Jesus did not fail to teach about *Elohim* in His Great Commission in His own words to the disciples "baptizing them in the name of the Father and of the Son and of the Holy Spirit" (Matthew 28:19, 20 NKJV). Hence, *God in three persons yet one God is* unmistakably biblical.

Jesus also uses baptism to identify Himself as the Son of God. Despite the fact that baptism is a one-time act, Jesus sends His disciples to baptize His followers as a sign to identify that a person is now coming out of the heathen life and taking his stand with Him and that this should be done in the name of *God the Father, the Son and the Holy Spirit.* This is a statement of faith that a person believes in God as the true Father of Jesus Christ and that Jesus is the true Son of God, the Savior of the world, and the belief that the Holy Spirit is the Comforter and the Counselor of those who come to believe and accept Jesus Christ as Lord and Savior. There is therefore the commitment made here to follow God as revealed by God the Father, the Son and the Holy Spirit. For instance, Jesus said "All things are delivered unto me of my Father: and no man knoweth the Son, but the Father; neither knoweth any man the Father, save the Son, and he to whomsoever the Son will reveal him" (Matthew 11:27 KJV). Here Jesus is making a declaration, that the Father had delivered into

His hands all power, authority, and judgment. *"They are delivered over or committed to me of My Father"*; meaning the whole administration of God's Kingdom has been given to Jesus Christ, God's Son. Jesus Christ receives everything from the Father, and in consequence of His union with the eternal God becomes the Lord, sovereign, and dispenser of all things. All the springs of the divine favor are in the hands of Christ, as Priest of God, and atoning sacrifice for men: all good proceeds from Him, as Savior, Mediator, Head, Pastor, and sovereign judge of the whole world. Jesus however emphasizes that people are blind to the truth, and that those who say they are wise in their own eyes shall not see the truth, but only babes; that is, those who are needful will have the truth revealed to them. If Muslims, Jews and atheists are humble enough in their hearts and become like children (babes), He is likely to reveal Himself to them. No doubt, many humble Muslims have seen Jesus in dreams, and some have seen Him personally because they humbled themselves and prayed to Him purposely to have the truth revealed to them.

Jesus also talks of things that are His in relation to God and all that God has given to Him. He said to the disciples "All things that the Father hath are mine: therefore, said I that He shall take of Mine, and shall show it to you" (John 16:15 KJV). We see here the phenomenal claim of Jesus that all that God the Father has is His. That means He is the Son of God and the Son of the Father. Here Jesus is declaring that there is perfect unity in the Godhead and that includes the Holy Spirit. The Holy Spirit here is commissioned to glorify Jesus Christ by making Him known to the world. He said, *"He (the Holy Spirit) shall take of mine, and show it to you"*. The Holy Spirit sent in the name of Jesus was to proclaim Jesus alone, that those who believe in Him will be saved. All things of the Father are the things of the Son, of Jesus Christ Himself. These include things shown and declared by the Holy Spirit. It means that the blessings of grace and the whole salvation package, which the Father has in store for His chosen more especially meant to reveal and apply the peculiar work of the Holy Spirit. In these, Jesus Christ is equally concerned with the Father: therefore, He said, *"I (He) shall take of mine, and shall show it unto you"*. Here Jesus does not mention that the things of God, His Father, are only His own, nor was there any necessity for it, because whatever is His, is the Father's, and whatever God His Father has is His. These are jointly concerned in everything relating to the salvation, benefit, comfort, and happiness of those who have come to believe in Jesus; so that when the Holy Spirit of God takes of the things of the one, He takes of the things of the other, and discovers, and applies them to the believer.

The key explanation to the above is that, God the Father and God the Son are represented in the Scripture as having agreed together in a covenant respecting the salvation of the human race. It was in this agreement that God the Father made over all the blessings that He had unto Jesus Christ. Therefore, Jesus has donatives and hereditary right as God's Son and Heir, as well as the Savior of the world. That further explains that when Jesus says that all things that the Father has are His, He speaks in the person of the Mediator from whom all *fullness* of life must draw out from (John 1:16 NKJV). The word *"fullness"* means that which fills, which also means the sum total of all that is in God. For God was pleased to have all His fullness dwell in Him (Col.1:19 NKJV). All the fullness of God was in Jesus Christ before He came to the earth and it continued to be with Him whilst He was on earth and it shall continue to be with throughout all eternity. Jesus Himself is the wisdom, the power, the glory, sanctification, righteousness and redemption of God (1 Cor. 1:24, 30). Christ is all these things to those who believe in Him. Due to Christ, the Holy Spirit can bear in us the fruit of Christlikeness which includes love, joy, peace, kindness, patience, self-control, goodness, faithfulness, gentleness (Gal.5:22 NKJV). These make us complete in Jesus Christ. So that through *one blessing after another,* He gives us grace enough to meet all our needs, no matter the circumstances or prevailing situation, His eyes are always kept on us. All that God the Father has belongs equally to Jesus Christ the Son, because the Father and the Son are One.

In short, Jesus Christ speaks of His riches, which He invites us to enjoy, and reckons the Holy Spirit among the gifts which we receive from the Father by His own hand. The Muslims and Jews deceive themselves, and that is because they bypass Christ, and go out of the way to seek God through other channels. The Jews and Muslims think that when they perform regularly specific rituals, e.g. when they face a particular direction to pray or when they wear the prescribed attire and eat prescribed types of food; and in the case of the Muslims, if they do more good works than bad, they will discover the God of the universe and enter heaven. The Bible declares that in Jesus dwells all the fullness of God; he is also the Lamb of God who takes away the sins of the world. Jesus Christ is the only atonement for sin that God accepts from everyone who wants to come to God as child, friend and true worshipper. There is no amount of work that we do that can please God, except what is given to us in the name of Jesus through His Spirit. In the name of Jesus every knee should bow, in heaven and on earth and under the earth (Philippians 2:10 NKJV). God has destined every knee to bow down to Christ and nothing shall be exempt. If we fail to look to Christ and look any other way, we only miss the way to God. Everything, no matter in which direction we pray, how many times we pray a day, what we eat or wear or whatever we do, if done outside Jesus Christ, will not help our journey towards genuine salvation and spiritual fulfilment. Christ has received from the Father everything He communicates to us by the Holy Spirit. The Holy Spirit therefore gives us the highest of all revelations which is revealing Jesus Christ to the world as, the Son of God, who is greater than the angels, and who, having completed the work of redemption, sits at God's right hand.

Men may not acknowledge that Jesus is the Son of God, but demons do. Whilst it is a problem for the world to know and accept Jesus as the Son of God, demons even bear testimony that Jesus is indeed God's Son. An evil spirit that possessed a man when he had seen Jesus, shouted, "What business do we have with each other, Jesus, Son of God Most High? I implore you by God, do not torment me!" (Mark 5:7 NKJV). The man who was possessed by the demon acknowledged Jesus as the Son of God and begged Him not to torment him by sending him back to hell. The evil spirit stricken with the power, purity and holiness of Jesus thought that Jesus was to destroy him before his time. According to the Bible, *"demons believe there is one God and they tremble"* (James 2:19 NKJV). As for the atheist, there is nothing called *belief* that is of value to him. Demons, however, believe that there is a God and that puts fear into them (James. 2:19). Therefore, if Muslims or Jews say they believe in God that alone is not enough. Why? Because even demons also believe there is a God and to them the belief in the deity of Jesus Christ as God is so real and so strong that it makes them afraid. That means there is no authentic and saving life in any belief that does not involve Jesus Christ. It is only a belief that leads a person to salvation through the Lord Jesus Christ that is a genuine belief. James continued in the next verse (20): "you foolish man, do you want evidence that faith without deeds is useless?" That makes true living faith a faith that works, a faith that really stirs a person to live a genuine life for Jesus Christ; which means a life that is pure and righteous and reaching a lost and desperate world with the message of salvation about Jesus Christ. If therefore even demons and evil spirits themselves, being the arch enemies of God, affirm that Jesus Christ is the Son of God, then we have greater evidence to testify to Muslims and Jews that Jesus is indeed, what He claims to be. This is The Christ, who existed before all things and before whom all religious and secular theories (including evolutionism, big bang, etc.) crumble and lose their validity (John 1:2, Colossians 1:17-20 NKJV), became man and God, through Him, has adopted and included us in the divine identity of Christ as the children of God (Ephesians 1:4-11 NKJV).

Furthermore, Jesus demonstrate to us the importance of the work He does in relation to the Father. He said: "My Father is always at His work" (JOHN 5:17 NIV) meaning "My father keeps on working even until now." The Jews were angry with Jesus because He worked miracles on the Sabbath day. Jesus answered them that His Father never stop working, even on the Sabbath day which is Sunday for Christians. When God created the world, the Bible mentions He rested on the seventh day. This means He rested from His creative work and not from His other work that also include love, mercy, compassion and looking and taking care of the universe. Jesus told them, since my Father is working, "I too am working" (John 5:17 (NIV) meaning that Jesus could do good on the Sabbath day just as His Father does good every day. In this example, Jesus was claiming to have the same right to work even as His Father works to erase the effect of the sins and the evil laws of men and to establish God's compassionate laws on earth. It is up to Muslims, the Jews and the atheists to accept the claim Jesus makes that He is equal with God or reject the claim. There is no middle ground for any of these three groups to stand. For the claim, concerning Jesus has been made and it is true, so the Muslims, the Jews and the atheists are forced to make their own decision whether to accept Jesus as their savior or not.

Lastly, one other thing that underscores the belief that Jesus is the Christ the Son of God is the life-changing message He gives to the individual and the very rock upon which the Church is founded. Jesus said in the words that followed Peters confession of faith, "On this rock I will build my church and the powers of death shall not prevail against it" (Mathew 16:18 NKJV). The confession of Peter was the foundation of the Christian church. Peter was the first to have grasped who Jesus really was and that was because he was the first to have confessed that Jesus is the Christ, *the Son of the living God*. Many were those that had been with Jesus earlier, but none of them had been with Jesus long enough to fully understand what it really meant by the *Son of God*. Peter who, later was to betray His Master through fear, understood it better and fully knew who Jesus was. Peter was the first leader of the nucleus of the Christian church which was founded by Christ and he was the one who preached the first sermon of the church on the day of Pentecost when three thousand souls were saved (Acts 2:41 NKJV). Jesus said to him: *"And I tell you that you are Peter, and on this rock I will build my church, and the gates of Hades will not overcome it"* (Mathew 16:18 NIV). That means that the Rock upon which the church is built is not Peter himself but His declaration that Christ is the Son of the living God. The church therefore consists of all those who acknowledge that Jesus Christ is the Son of the living God and are therefore willing to serve

Him. Besides being the Rock upon which the church is founded Jesus Christ is also the builder the power that is behind the church (1 Cor. 3:11). After Pentecost when Peter had first built the church, Jesus Christ who is the solid foundation of the church now holds the church together. As already pointed out the church includes, from the viewpoint of Jesus, everyone who truly believes and confesses that He is the Christ, the Son of the living God. Jesus is saying that hell could not contain Him and likewise it will not contain the Church and those called to belong to Him will not be absorbed by hell. Jesus is also saying that the Church will never die, and He further gives us hope that the rock upon which the Church is built will proclaim liberty to the captives and set free those who are bound (Isaiah 61:1 NKJV).

Jesus shows His love to the church after He had resurrected from the dead and gone back to God. He said to God "And now I am no more in the world, but these are in the world, and I come to thee Holy Father, keep through thine own name those whom thou hast given me, that they may be one, as we are" (John 17:11 KJV). This did not mean Jesus and God did not love the world. They do, that was why Jesus came to die to save the world from perishing (John 3:16 NKJV). What Jesus sees is a divisive world that threatens the church. It was possible that His followers be influenced by such divisiveness and be led astray. Therefore, He prayed to His Father to keep them together in unity. He prayed for His disciples because they belong to the Father. He had to pray for them that His Father would give them special strength in the days ahead. We see here that the disciples belong to both the Father and Jesus. Jesus informs us: "All I have is yours, and all you have is mine" (John 17:10 NIV). That means they belong to both of them. God is concerned about every Christian as well as Jesus Christ; therefore, Jesus can surely count on God the Father who hears the prayers of all Christians who pray in the name of Jesus. This is seen in the lives of the disciples who lived for Jesus, for their lives brought glory to Him. They lived for Jesus and showed loyalty and allegiance to Him by proclaiming to the world the truth about Him as the Savior of the world and the Lord of the universe.

Jesus was thereby glorified, honored, and praised. For that reason, Jesus prayed for them that they might become strong in their lives as they live to witness for Him for the salvation of perishing souls. Jesus was concerned that those who follow Him shall be in need of assistance and support, and that His intercession and assistance so that they will be kept in the truth. The whole mission of preaching the Gospel to the world rests on their shoulders and depends on their faithfulness and endurance. Therefore, in this last hour before He went to Heaven, Jesus prayed for them with the intensity, asking God to keep them together as one. God the Holy Spirit was to take over, as He leaves the world. The Holy Spirit therefore came and made His abode on earth among His disciples and He is at present in the world revealing Jesus to millions of people before the end comes. As a final phase in this revelation of the Lord Jesus we shall examine his position as the God of the Universe.

11. Unveiling Jesus Christ, the God of the Universe

11.1 Various attempts to refute Jesus as God

Today, many scholars having studied the history and the myth surrounding Jesus Christ, have come to the convincing proof that Jesus Christ is God. People in the days of Jesus and records of testimonies from Jesus himself have staggered people by what He said and did. Jesus would be walking down the road with His disciples and then would make certain comments: "before Abraham was, I am (John 8:58 KJV); "he who has seen Me has seen the Father" (John 14:9 NKJV). It is interesting to listen to some of the comments from the contemporary world, from people of different thoughts and backgrounds which argue for against the issue of whether Jesus Christ is God or not. Is Jesus Christ God? Some argue that Jesus never explicitly said: "I *am God*" Jesus never used the exact words, *I am God* neither did He state explicitly "*I am a man,* or *a prophet.*" On the other hand, He did continually refer to Himself in ways that perplexed His listeners.

Whilst both the Bible and the Quran confirm that Jesus Christ is God incarnated in the flesh, in Islam, it is an unforgivable sin for a Muslim to believe that Jesus Christ is God. This is legitimate since Moslems believe Islam to be the only saving religion (Quran 3:19, 85). This position can be accepted only at a high cost to the

Christian faith as this contradicts the mystery that surrounds the birth, death and resurrection of Jesus Christ and His ascension to heaven. Islam denies the reliability of the Christian Scripture, which contradicts the Quran on at least three key issues: *God's holy Trinity, the uniqueness of Jesus Christ* and *God's power supernaturally demonstrated in the death and resurrection of Christ.* These are the central issues of the contention between Christians and Muslims, for Muslims say Jesus is not God. There are people who said the same thing about Jesus not being God, but later came to believe that Jesus is indeed God. An example is C. S. Lewis. Lewis initially considered Jesus a myth and investigated the evidence about Jesus and was finally convinced that not only was Jesus real, but He was unlike any man that ever lived on the face of the earth. C. S. Lewis wrote concerning Jesus: *"Then comes the real shock, among these Jews there suddenly turns up a man who goes about talking as if He was God. He claims to forgive sins. He says He always existed. He says He is coming to judge the world at the end of time."*(18) Lewis thought the claim of Jesus to be God were too radical and profound because Jesus happened to be just an ordinary teacher of religion. Lewis confirmed that Jesus was a great moral teacher but was not prepared to accept His claim to be God (21). In his quest for the truth, Lewis realized he could not have it both ways with the identity of Jesus, that He was either God in the flesh or that His claims were false. Moreover, if He were false, it was either Jesus would be lying intentionally or is a lunatic with a God complex. Jesus wouldn't have lied for the benefit of Himself or anyone else, since many believers chose to be martyred rather than renounce His Lordship. It was true the Jewish opponents of His day tried to expose Him as a fraud or a liar and barraged Him with questions just to trap Him to contradict Himself. Yet Jesus all the time responded with remarkable consistency. There is no evidence in church history or in secular history that Jesus lied about anything. *"How in the name of logics, common sense and experience could a deceitful, selfish, depraved man have invented, and consistently maintained from the beginning to end, the purest and noblest character known in history with the most perfect air of truth and reality"*, said Philip Schaff (Philip Schaff 23). To go with the option of lie seems to go against everything that Jesus lived, taught and died for. Lewis concludes in *Mere Christianity* that Jesus is exactly who He claimed to be. This made Lewis, the great literary genius, to renounce his former atheism to become a committed Christian.

11.2 A former Muslims testifies that Jesus is God

In order to help Muslims to understand more about the nature of Jesus Christ, we will shortly address the testimony of a former Muslim student who wanted to become an Imam. To hide his identity, I have chosen to call him Martin. According to Martin, whilst he was working in a Muslim mosque as an Imam and a parish priest in India, he proclaimed to the Muslim community that Jesus Christ is not God. His reasons were that God was only Allah, and Allah never got married, and it was impossible for Allah to have a son or sons. He preached and taught his listeners, that *Jesus Christ is not God*. This is a popular message in the Muslim community in India, as they themselves do not believe that Jesus Christ is God. This is the same message preached and taught by Imams in the Muslim communities to Muslims at a very tender age, and Muslims are brought up to believe that Jesus Christ is not the Son of God and not God. Since Islam is compulsory for the people living in most of the Muslim nations, it is a crime to become a Christian or preach Christianity. In countries where it is a crime to preach Christianity, it is difficult for people to find out the truth about Jesus Christ. That means very important religious knowledge outside the scope of the Quran can be difficult to access as a basis of independent judgment and choice. Persons are prevented from reaching out to useful sources of information once indoctrinated. This makes it difficult to make a decisive choice when it comes to choosing between Prophet Mohammed and Jesus Christ. The Imams hinder students of the Quran to find the truth themselves about Jesus. The Imams and teachers of the Quran have become the mouthpiece of the people, who impart knowledge deemed as final without question or consideration. Therefore, since there is no religious democracy in Islam, it is very difficult for students of the

Quran to have the freedom to read the Bible without facing death penalty. If truly Christians and Muslims serve the same God, why do the authorities of the Muslim nations not to allow Bibles into their nations? Qurans are for sale on bookshelves in nations around the world that openly proclaim Christ. What will happen if nations of Islam permit the Bible to be on sale openly in Islam-dominated nations like Saudi Arabia? The reader can judge that for himself. Perhaps it is not a public crime to read the Bible in India but judging from the experience of some Christian converts in Muslim families, severe punishments await those who read in the Bible in Muslim homes. We hear of Muslims and Hindus in India and elsewhere who have tortured and killed Christians for their faith in Jesus. We have also heard of conflicts between Muslims and Hindus that have resulted in the death of some people. What legacies are those involved in religious violence leaving behind for the generations to come, and what benefit does one gain from such an experience? Nothing else but vanity (Ecclesiastics 1:12-14; Mark 8:36 NKJV).

Martin continued that whilst he was teaching people that Jesus Christ is not God, a student asked him, *"If you are saying that Jesus is not God, then who is Jesus"?* This was a homework for him, for he did not know the answer. He therefore decided to go back to the Quran to find out what the Quran says about Jesus. According to him, he went back to read the entire Quran with the motive to find out all about Jesus. He had earlier read the entire Quran, which he said consists of 114 chapters, but this time he read it carefully taking note of everything about Jesus. After reading the entire Quran, he found out that the name of Prophet Mohammad appears at only four places, but he was surprised to find the name of Jesus in 25 places. He said he became confused and asked himself *"Why the Quran gives more preference to Jesus"?* Secondly, he said he could not see any woman's name in the Quran not even Prophet Mohammad mother's name, or wife's name apart from Mariam, or Mary the mother of Jesus. According to Martin, Chapter three of Quran is entitled *"the family of Mariam"*. Quoting Quran chapter 3 verse 34 onwards it says that Mary was born without the original sin, and she never committed any sin in her life, and she was a virgin. Martin mentioned that in Quran chapter 50 verses 23, Mary went to heaven with her physical body.

According to Martin after he had read what the Quran says about Jesus in chapter 3 from verses 45 to 55, he discovered 10 points that the Quran makes about Jesus. He mentioned that the first thing the Quran says is *kallimatulli*, which in Arabic means *the Word of* God and second thing is *ahimokuli* which means *Spirit of God* and the third is (*isa masi*) which means *Jesus Christ*. Therefore, the Quran gives the names for Jesus as *"The Word of God, Spirit of God, and Jesus Christ"*. Again, Martin in his discovery mentioned that the Quran says Jesus spoke when he was two days old and created a bird with mud and gave it life. He said Jesus took some mud, formed a bird, then breathed into it, and it became a live bird. He said with this discovery from the Quran, he knew Jesus could give life. Again, he said the Quran mentioned that Jesus cured a man born blind and a man with leprosy and gave life to dead people. Martin concluded his findings that the Quran says Jesus went to heaven and that He is still alive and will come again.

After Martin had found out the truth about Jesus in the Quran, he wanted to know what the Quran says about Mohammad. According to him, the Quran says Prophet Mohammad is not the *Word of God,* not the *Spirit of God* and that he never spoke when he was two days old, and he never created any bird with mud to give it life, and never cured any sick people, nor raised any dead person. He emphasized that prophet Mohammed himself died, and that according to Islam he is not alive, and he will not come back. Martin found out there are differences between these two prophets, *Jesus and Mohammed*. He said as a devout Muslim, he never called Jesus *God,* and had concluded that Jesus is *a prophet,* but that He is *a prophet greater than Mohammad*. He became confused about what he found in the Quran, so he went to his teacher, the one who taught him for ten years in Arabic college, and asked him, *"teacher, how did God create the universe"*? His teacher answered that God created the universe through, *"The Word of God"*. He then interrogated his Imam by asking: *The Word*, is it a

Creator or Creation? He wanted his teacher to answer whether *The Word of God* is a Creator or Creation, for he has just read that the Quran says Jesus is the *"The Word of God"* and the *"Spirit of God"* (Quran Chapter 5). According to him, if his teacher says the *Word of God is Creator,* which naturally will mean that *Jesus is the Creator,* then Muslims must become Christians, and supposing his teacher says the *Word is Creation* then the teacher would be trapped. Martin, a devoted Muslim at that time confirms that the Quran says, *everything was created through The Word.* He continued; supposing the teacher said the *Word is Creation,* then how did God create *The Word?* According to him, his teacher could not say *The Word* is *Creator,* or *Creation* but that the *"Word"* means creation, and not God. Martin said the Imam could not explain the difference between the Word being the Creator or Creation and that though the Quran confirms what the Bible says, the Imam said the explanation does not mean *The Word* is God. He said his teacher was quite angry and pushed him out of his room and said, *"The Word is not God, and not Creator nor Creation, you get out of here",* he concluded. Sadly enough, the Imam who was supposed to be his teacher and to know better became angry and only pushed him out.

In concluding his investigations about Jesus in the Quran, Martin emphasized that the reason why Muslims don`t want to become Christians is because they have been blinded with the wrong teachings from their priests, the Imams. If the Quran talks about Jesus as *"The Word of God"* and as the *"Spirit of God"*, then automatically the two statements make Jesus automatically *"God"*. The logic is that, these two words: *The Word of God* and *the Spirit of God* are titles of God, and no ordinary human being gets these titles except God. Martin described his Imam, the Arabic scholar and teacher as unlearned, blind, arrogant, and a person not ready to learn. He said that of other Imams and teachers who claim to be scholars of the Quran that they live in deception and arrogance. Martin pointed out that all the Muslim Imams and teachers have been teaching that *"The Word"* is not Creator, nor Creation, and not God, even though the Quran testifies clearly in black and white that *"Jesus is The Word* of God" and that *The Word of God* created all things. At the close of his investigation, Martin mentioned that if the Imams say *The Word* cannot be equal with *God*; then that should be their own problem. Martin made the following remarks to his teacher: "if you say that The Word is not the Creator or the Creation that is the reason why Christians say: "*The Word is the Son of God*". Interestingly enough, the learned Imam replied: "*if there is a son of God, Martin must show him the wife of God, because without a wife there is no chance of having a son*". Martin then showed the Imam a portion from the Quran that says that God can see without eyes, God can talk without tongue and God can hear without ears. He told the Imam, if God is able to do all these things, then it is possible for God to have a child without a wife. He then took his Quran, and put it on his chest, and said *"Allah, tell me what I should do because your Quran says Jesus is still alive, and Mohammad is no more. Tell me whom should I accept."* Martin wanted God to prove that what he had just discovered was the truth and he needed confirmation for that. When he had prayed and opened the Quran, the place he found was *chapter 10 verse 94*. To his surprised he found the following writing: *If you have any doubt in this Quran which I give to you, go and read the Bible, or ask the people who read the Bible.* It might be obvious that the prophet Mohammed might have got most of his original messages that were inscribed into the Quran from either the Jews or the Christians, mostly the Catholics. The Catholics believe that Mary ascended to heaven when she died. This is a typical doctrine of Catholicism embraced by Mohammed from the Catholics and many other examples that as seen in the Quran.

Looking at the testimony of Martin, it means Prophet Mohammed of Islam could be wrong or uncertain about most of the things he personally wrote concerning the Bible. It is quite confusing to affirm that Muslims should consult the Jews or the Christians if they are in doubt of certain things and then go ahead to disagree with certain doctrines of the Bible or for that matter the Torah. Martin therefore testifies to all Muslims about the truth regarding Jesus and begged them to give their lives to Jesus Christ. He affirmed that Jesus is the only way to the kingdom of God. He said to Muslims *"please don't perish like other Muslims serving the god they do not know"*. Who is the God they do not know? Martin stated that in the Quran, all human beings are slaves to Allah and Allah is always the Master. He mentions, *"Allah is the Master and the Master can't love the slave and the slave can't love the Master"*. That is because Allah expects *total submission* and a person cannot obey some laws and disobey others whilst he has different opinion from that of Allah. That makes it impossible to serve Allah completely since no human being is perfect and not one person on the earth can obey all the laws of Allah. Martin therefore extends a welcome hand to his fellow Muslims to allow Jesus into their lives as their Lord and their God.

Martin told of the most painful part of his life experience; that his father tried to kill him after he accepted Jesus Christ as his Lord and Savior. According to him, he was chained and locked up to die from starvation. Eventually on the day that his father tried to kill him, he shouted the name of *Jesus!* All of a sudden instead of the knife cutting him, it turned around from the father's own hand to cut deep into the stomach of the father instead. The father screamed for help as he fell flat on the ground. It was in such a dramatic state that Martin was able to escape. He is now living in Europe and now a Pastor and Missionary of the Lord Jesus Christ. What a powerful testimony for all Moslems not hardened in the heart to learn from and to take home with them to save their entire homes and families.

In line with the above testimony, there are many Imams as well as Jewish Rabbis who know the absolute truth about the Word of God and can truly testify about Jesus Christ, that He is not an ordinary human being, but will not give this a second thought. It is, however, unfortunate that most of the so-called men of God have arrogantly stood against the truth and true knowledge of Jesus Christ as the Son of God and God. Most of them, because of prejudices and the positions they hold, have done so consciously just to protect their pockets and stomachs. Just like Pharaoh King of Egypt in the Bible who would not relent to let the people of Israel go, these spiritual leaders of both the Muslim and Jewish people, have hopelessly locked up their hearts and refused to open them to those they lead. They continue to protect their self-interest as teachers, rabbis and imams of the people. As the people continue to come to them, the Imams of the Muslims say to their students, *don't read the Bible, for it is corrupted.* They cherish their self-interest for the sake of the office they hold and for fear of losing the faith, trust and confidence the people have in them. This is a very dangerous position they have taken, as they will account for that before the God of all the earth.

11.3 Views of a Muslim Anti-Christ about Jesus' claim to being God

Against the backcloth of the testimony and the life experience of Martin, we question of whether Jesus Christ is God or not. As already mentioned, many Muslims refuse to accept the fact that Jesus Christ is God. We have read from chapter six about a very popular well-known Muslim teacher in India, Dr. Z (not his real name). Dr. Z. gives contrary teachings against the Christian belief that Jesus Christ is God and if we are able to show in the Bible where it is stated that Jesus Christ is God, he will change from Islam to become a Christian. Already Dr. Z has committed himself by saying he is a better Christian than most of the Christians. This same false teacher teaches Muslims in India that the Holy Spirit is the same as the Prophet Mohammed. One surprising fact about Dr. Z is how he is preoccupied with diluting the Christian message and the Bible, and not devoting his time to teach about his own religion. Anytime Dr. Z meets his audience, his favorite topic is the Christian Bible, in order to refuse the deity of Jesus Christ. Surprisingly enough, Dr. Z knows so many Bible quotations but has no ear to hear the voice of God.

The Bible describes such persons as antichrist (1 John 2:22; 4:3 NKJV). Any person who denies that Jesus Christ is the Messiah, the Son of God is a forerunner of the antichrist. First, he is a liar and secondly, he denies God the Father if he denies the Lord Jesus the Son. God did the greatest thing that could ever be done for man and that was to send His only Son into the world to save man by dying on the cross. If any man says that God did not send Jesus Christ to die for humanity, and that Jesus is not the Son of God, it means that person is denying both God and Jesus Christ. This is because all over the New Testament, it says repeatedly that Jesus Christ who is also known as the *"Word of God"* is the Son of God, and He is the One sent to reveal God to the world. More to this than expected, what more does the Quran say about *Jesus, the Word of God*?

11.4 The Quran testifies that Jesus is God

The Quran has a lot to say about *Jesus, the Word of God*. Taking the birth of Jesus for example, the Quran says, *"Christ Jesus the son of Mary (no more than) a messenger of Allah, and His Word, which He bestowed on Mary, and a Spirit proceeding from Him"* (Sura 4:171). It is hard to understand how Muslims themselves explain Sura 4:171 and interpreted what it means by *"a Spirit proceeded from Jesus"*. In simple English, if the Quran says what was bestowed upon Mary was the *Word,* then why are Muslims refusing to accept that *His Word*, which was bestowed upon Mary is Jesus Christ. Which simply means Mary conceived or became pregnant of *The Word,* which was bestowed upon her. The Bible confirms this by saying: "The angel answered, The Holy Spirit will come on you, and the power of the Most High will overshadow you. Therefore, the Holy One to be born will be called the Son of God" (Luke 1:35 NKJV). This concisely means the child or *the Holy One* is the *Word of God* conceived and born by the power of the Holy Spirit through the Virgin Mary. Referring to *"no more than a messenger of Allah"* in Sura 4:171 to Jesus implies Jesus is only a mere Messenger. However, in this same quotation, this same mere messenger seems to have significant power as Allah bestowed Him as His Word on Mary. In this development, even though the Quran says Jesus is a mere Messenger, it at the same time confirms that Jesus the son of Mary and His Word (either meaning God`s Word or Jesus Word) was bestowed upon Mary and a Spirit proceeding from Him (Him meaning either Jesus or God). This verse in the Quran distorts itself, however, talks and mixes up Jesus and God altogether in Sura 4:171). How then can we understand this better from the Biblical point of view?

We can get a gist of the above by looking at the revelation of John concerning *The Word of God*. The Apostle John opens our eyes with the following in his revelation: "in the beginning was the Word, and the Word was with God and the Word was God. He was in the beginning with God. All things were made through Him and without Him nothing was made that was made. In Him was life, and the life was the light of men" (John 1:1-4 NKJV). One needs to discern deeply to understand what this revelation means, for it is clear. John being Jewish had it difficult to write this to non-Jewish people since they had not heard of the word Messiah or Savior before. On the other hand, since the Messiah was the central idea in Christianity, John had to present this in such a way for Christians to understand. To make the meaning of the Messiah vivid, John used the *Word* which was easier for both the Jews and the Gentiles to understand. John made us understand that the *Word*, which is *Jesus Christ*, was the expression and the exact image of what God wanted to say to the world. Jesus was God's utterance and *God's Word* to humanity. In making the world, God took nothing but His will and power, and spoke *The Word* and created everything out of nothing.

Going back to the Quran, the Spirit that came upon Mary was not Jesus as the Quran tries to make us believe. Rather it is the Holy Spirit, which is the Spirit of God (Sura 4:171). Under the Trinity, we have God the Father, God the Son and the Holy Spirit. When the Quran talks about *The Word*, it is talking about *God the Son*, who is the same as *Jesus Christ*. Jesus is the Word of God as spoken by the Prophets and confirmed by the Bible. Interestingly enough, the Quran says God has a Spirit and God has a Word (Sura 5:110). This makes our discussion of the Trinity true, interesting and authentic. To Muslims, *Sura 5:110* could be explained as follows: *God is God, God has a Son who is Jesus Christ, and God has a Spirit called the Holy Spirit, thus the Trinity.* That is easier to understand if one does not close his eyes to prejudice.

11.5 The Bible Testifies that Jesus is God

There are also other Scriptures from the Bible that concisely identify Jesus as God. For example, following the visitation of Jesus after His resurrection, the disciples tell Thomas, *we have seen the Lord*. Thomas after seeing Jesus upon the second visitation said to Him, *"My Lord and My God"* (John 20:24-28 NKJV). Thomas had not been with the disciples when Jesus first appeared to them. Initially when he was told that Jesus had been with them, he refused to believe that Jesus had really risen from the dead, for he had not seen Him with his own naked eyes. The statement used by Thomas after he had seen Jesus includes the verb of sight: *Unless I see Him*. That is, touch with my hands the print of the nails ... I will not believe (John. 20:25 NKJV). The refusal of Thomas to believe, despite the confession of the other disciples, made his condition so clear and absolute. In his situation, there is the need for personal verification that is directed by sight and accessible by eye contact and nothing less. Thomas said: "Unless I see in His hands the print of the nails and put my finger into the print of the nails, and put my hand into His side, I will not believe" (John 20:25 NKJV). We see Thomas making his own individual examination and that includes his personal direct seeing of the visible marks of the crucifixion and even the touching of those marks, which is an absolute condition and a non-negotiable term for believing. What is worthy of note is that the disciples' affirmation that they have seen the Lord is treated with utter skepticism and rejection. Apart from that there is also an unyielding attitude of his situation, where believing seems to be unthinkable, without first seeing the Lord, or without having direct physical contact as evidence and verification. To confirm His resurrection and to prove that He is God, Jesus visited the disciples the second time. This time Thomas was around, and upon recognizing Jesus, he testified that it was Him. Thomas now acknowledged Jesus as his Lord and God and therefore his statement of confession: My Lord and my God (John 20:28 NIV).

The name *God* is expressly given to Christ in His own presence and by one of His own apostles in the presence of the others who all together saw the resurrected Jesus Christ. This confession most likely, made Thomas to drop on his knees acknowledging Jesus as God. Thomas now knew that Jesus was truly risen from the dead and that all that Jesus had said and done were true and that Jesus is both Lord and God, likewise the Sovereign Majesty of the universe (1 Cor. 8:6 NKJV). The declaration from Thomas as an eyewitness is considered a clear proof of the resurrected Christ, that He is divine. This is one of the many examples that the Bible gives to prove that Jesus Christ is God. Unfortunately, skeptics would not accept these proofs and contend that the Bible does not have sufficient evidence about the deity of Christ.

11.6 Debate between Muslim and Christian scholars about the Deity of Christ

The subject of Jesus Christ's deity has brought about several debates between Muslims and Christians. During one of the debates, an Islamic scholar Sheikh Joe (not his real name) claimed that Jesus Christ is not God. In reference to the exclamation made by Thomas: *My God,* Sheik Joe says the exclamation of Thomas *My God,* was just a sign of astonishment, and that we use such exclamation everyday while talking to people. He cited the following example: I see John cutting his wrist with a Rambo knife and upon seeing John I exclaim: My God, John what are you doing? Sheik Joe asked, do I mean that John is God? Sheikh Joe removed the *"and"* and put his own words like "My God, my Lord" and end by saying that Thomas was not claiming that Jesus was his (1) *God* and (2) *Lord.* This time he brings the *"and"*; thus *"my Lord and my God".* In daily parlance, it is rare that people make such proclamation by putting the two words *My Lord and My God* together at the same time when they want to show astonishment. In everyday conversation, it is very unlikely that John will cut his wrist with a knife and someone will make an utterance *My God and My Lord, John what are you doing?* This would be rather an uncommon exclamation in everyday conversation.

In the Biblical context, there is no comma (,). When you remove the comma from the example of Sheikh Joe, you end up calling John *"Lord"* and *"God"* – thus my Lord and My God John. The main strength in this argument lies on the passage at hand without having to invoke other passages to explain away the grammar. Thomas is affirming two things here, that Jesus is both his Lord and his God. What about the response Jesus made to Thomas? Sheikh Joe is painting a blind picture to the Muslim world and only to protect his religious interest and his position as Sheik. There is something important to note here. Carefully, the confession of faith made by Thomas in this situation assigns to Jesus the attributes of Lord and God. This is the same attributes used in the Old Testament for Yahweh, the One and only God of the Jewish people. Thomas addresses Jesus the same way the Israelites addressed Yahweh as God. Is it not remarkable that the skeptical Thomas, an unbelieving disciple of Jesus, confesses and declares his faith in support of what the Scripture declares that "In the beginning was the Logos, and the Logos was with God, and the Logos was God" (John 1:1 NKJV). The Logos became flesh and dwelt among us (John 1:14 NKJV), and that He was crucified and risen, and is now acknowledged as *Lord and God* (John 20:28 NKJV).

The confession of Thomas, after he had seen the resurrected Lord, constitutes an advance form of faith which no other person can testify more than the witness himself, the witness being Thomas the doubter. The first part of the statement of Thomas "my Lord", is taken either as a question or as recognition of a fact, speaking of believing in the risen Lord, because he has seen Him. One cannot doubt that Jesus clearly speaks of a faith that cannot be taken for granted. This is a faith that results from visual and sight experience. This is so convincing that there exists no other critical explanation to give than what is given in these examples. The statement applied by Jesus also poses a different type of faith that does not need to depend on visual experiences. When Jesus heard the confession of Thomas, He then addresses Thomas: "Because you have seen me, you have believed. Blessed are those who have not seen and (yet) have believed" (John 20:29 NIV).

Another important fact about Jesus being God is captured in the book of Romans which says: "of whom are the fathers and from whom, according to the flesh, Christ came, who is over all, the eternally blessed God. Amen" (Romans 9:5 NKJV). The King James Version says: "Whose are the fathers, and of whom as concerning the flesh Christ came, who is over all, God blessed forever. Amen." Although the exact wording of the above translations differs, they are worded to make Christ into God. The Jews had the privilege of the Messiah coming from their heritage. Their ancestors had been the primary recipients of the promise of the Messiah coming from their roots. This was a covenant promised between God and man. It was the most glorious privilege of the Jews. Paul writing to the Romans declares the deity and humanity of Jesus Christ, that He came as a man, but that He is God over all and forever blessed. God's blessings to the Jews, who have a heritage of being aggressively monotheistic was to give the Jews the best inheritance among all the nations of the world. Since the Jews have refused to accept the Gospel Paul was preaching; Paul who was trying to win them for Jesus Christ calls them "my kindred in the flesh" (v. 3), and says he has sorrow in his heart for them (v. 2). Paul does not put into this section a phrase that would be offensive to the very people he is trying to win. We see in other Biblical references that the Christ the Apostle wrote and preached about was *fully* God (Phil. 2:6; Titus 2:13 NKJV) and *fully man* (Gal. 4:4; 2 Tim. 2:8 NKJV).

There were times in the past when heresies dominated the church, some of which were the accounts of Gnostic knowledge. Paul therefore took stand to correct most of the untrue and confusing statements from heresies and constantly presented a clear picture of ideas to the two natures of Christ, man and God. Paul was all the time filled with the Holy Spirit when he wrote the epistles. In Romans 9:5, there is a contrast between the human origins and the deity of Christ. However, some ambiguity exists in the punctuation of the phrase "*according to the flesh who is over all God*". To whom does the phrase refer? Does this refer to God the Father or Christ? Paul would not call Christ *"God"* without giving any explanation and he would do so the more on any subject that presents Christ as God. Paul wept over Israel feeling deep sorrows for his own people who although had Jewish privileges, had rejected the true Messiah. In this context, not only did the Messiah come from Jewish stock but also is a universal King who will be eternally worshipped as God. In addition, the phrase *"over all"* denotes ultimate supremacy. Jesus the Messiah is supreme ruler over all Jews, Gentiles, believers, and unbelievers including all the prophets who had come. It is true that the Scripture calls God the Father *"over all"* (Eph. 4:6 NKJV). That means we owe God more than we could ever pay. The reason is that God has taken His own dear Son and provided the Ideal and Perfect righteousness for us. In addition, He has provided a Substitute not only to die for us but also to actually bear our punishment for having rejected and rebelled against Him. We even went to the extent of cursing God and breaking His laws. In spite of that, God provided deliverance from death and provided a new life for us in Jesus Christ through the Holy Spirit. Finally, God provided an absolute assurance of everlasting life with Him in Heaven forever and ever.

Whilst the scripture calls God the Father *"over all"* Jesus is also called *"over all."* Thus, the Scripture reads, "The word which He sent to the sons of Israel, preaching peace through Jesus Christ "He is Lord of all" (Acts 10:36 NKJV). Note the parallel to the phrase in Romans 9:5: *"who is over all God"* with the end of Acts 10:36: *"He is of all Lord".* Further, in Romans, Paul states that Jesus is *Lord of all* (Romans 10:12 NKJV). God sent His Word to Israel as the first nation to receive God's word of salvation. The Word God sent was Jesus Himself, His own Son. The Bible says the Word came by Jesus Christ and even though the Word came to Israel, that was not meant for Israel alone. It is therefore clear that Jesus Christ did not come just for the salvation of the people of Israel alone, but for the whole world. The Bible therefore declares, *Christ is Lord of all.* Which means Christ was not only for the Jews but He is Lord of all the nations and that include the poor, the privileged, the heathen and all people who truly fear God and seek righteousness, and not the least Muslims and Jews and the atheists alike; He came for them all.

The Lordship of Jesus Christ over all things is also expressed where Jesus is named as Creator of all things (Col. 1:16-17 NKJV). Jesus Christ created all things for Himself. If indeed He did create all things, then to whom would creation look and which among creation would worship, praise and grant Him the entire honor that is due Him? It is obvious that creation would look to its Creator by finding its end and consummation in Jesus Christ. Jesus Christ therefore created the universe that it might be His to love, bless, save and redeem. Creation therefore owes its praise, honor, worship and service to the Lord Jesus Christ. The whole world, at the corner of every nation, in the cities and villages Christians all over the world sing praises and worship Jesus Christ for the great work of redemption done for humanity on the cross. This is because Jesus Christ is Lord overall and He is before all things. He is not created, but the Creator. Nothing was in existence when He created the world. Before the beginning of time, and before the universe ever came into being, He was there. He is "God over all things and the Lord of all and the Creator of all things" (1 Cor. 2:8 NKJV). It is true that in the New Testament Paul normally refers to the Father as *"God"* and the Son as *Lord*, particularly when the Father and Jesus appear in the same context. In many other examples, even though Paul regularly refers to the Father as *God,* he has specifically referred to Jesus as *the God* in Titus (Titus 2:13 NKJV); existing in the *nature of God* in Philippians (Philippians 2:6 NKJV); and dwelling in *all the fullness of Deity* in Colossians (Colossians 2:9 NKJV); and as mentioned, *the Creator of all things* in Colossians (Colossians 1:16-17 NKJV). To Paul, Jesus Christ is the *YHWH* of Isaiah (Isaiah 45:23 NKJV) and as presented in Philippians (Philippians 2:10-11 NKJV).

11.7 Jesus received worship as God

Another important factor that shows that Jesus Christ is God is His status to receive worship of man. Jesus made Pilate to understand

He has a Kingdom that is not of this world but of the heavenly and divine being. To the Christian, Jesus is *the King of Kings and the Lord of Lords*. To Muslims it is quite outrageous to call a man King of Kings and Lord of Lords. The Quran mentions in the Hadith that the most awful name in Allah's sight on the Day of resurrection, will be that of a man calling himself *"King of Kings"* (Hadith 8:73,224). Was it not another way to bring Jesus down, after He has been named as a mere messenger or Prophet or a man created like Adam? It is another offensive way to deny the divinity of Jesus as King of Kings by the author of the Quran. Jesus takes a stand to even affirm His status to Martha, just before He raised Lazarus from the dead. He said to her: "I am the resurrection and the life. Anyone who believes in me will live, even after dying" (John 11:25 NKJV). This is quite phenomenal, and Jesus is claiming that all life exists only by the will and power of Him Jesus. That means there is nothing existing apart from the will of Jesus Christ. Therefore, if a dead person wishes to live, only Jesus can give him life. Moreover, if a living person does not wish to die, only Jesus Christ can keep him from dying. If Jesus Himself is the resurrection and life, what would be the fate of those who fail to acknowledge Him as *King of Kings?*

Apart from rejecting the idea of Jesus being the King of Kings, the Quran pronounces death upon the enemies of the angel Gabriel. This is because it was the angel Gabriel who brought the message of the Quran by the permission of Allah and confirms that the Torah and the Bible of the Christians were the first guidance and glad tidings to believers. The Quran refutes the Kingship of Jesus Christ but praises the Jewish Torah and the Christian Bible. Jesus is the King of Kings and the Lord of Lords; therefore, He deserves to be worshipped. Muslims are not happy with Christians who worship Jesus because they say Jesus is not God but a man. There are several examples in the Bible where men refused to be worshipped because it was only meant for God. Cornelius fell down to worship Peter and Peter forbade it saying that he himself was just a man (Acts 10:25, 26 NKJV). The Apostle John after receiving the revelation from the angel of God sought to worship the angel, but the angel forbade it because he was a fellow servant and that only God could be worshipped (Revelation 22:8,9; 19:10 NKJV). People who worship and serve created things, rather than the Creator, have left the truth of God (Romans 1:25 NKJV). If man worships any created thing – whether man, angel, heavenly body, or some other object in nature constitutes idolatry. On the contrary, Jesus receives the unique worship God deserves. In the Scriptures, Jesus was often worshipped while He was on earth before His resurrection. There are several examples in the Bible where Jesus was worshipped. A leper came and worshipped Jesus after He had healed him (Matthew 8:2 NKJV). A ruler came worshipping Him because of his daughter who was sick, and Jesus followed him to his house (Mathew 9:18; Mark 5:6 NKJV). His disciples were afraid of the storms and after Jesus had calmed down the storm, the disciples worshipped Him saying He was the Son of God (Matthew 14:33 NKJV). After Jesus had healed the blind man, He revealed Himself to be the Son of God. The man said he believed, and he worshipped Jesus (John 9:35-38 NKJV). If Jesus were not God, but had been a mere man, messenger, or prophet on earth such religious worship would have been blasphemy and should have been forbidden by Jesus Himself as it was in the case of the angel of God (Rev.22:9 NKJV) and in the case of Peter (Acts 10:26 NKJV). The Bible also declares how created beings also worshipped Jesus after His resurrection (Matthew 28:9, 17; John 20:28, 29; Luke 24:52 NKJV) and even angels are instructed by God to worship Jesus (Hebrews 1:6 NKJV). This context of worship does not fit the idea of obeisance to earthly kings or rulers but only Jesus.

11.8 The Everlasting kingship of Jesus proves His Deity

Moreover, the future everlasting kingdom of God which is to be ruled by the Lord Jesus is an indubitable testimony that He is God. There is nothing on this earth that last forever, but the angel who visited Mary during the annunciation mentioned that Jesus shall establish a Kingdom which shall have no end, and that He will reign upon the throne of David, and that God Himself will place Him upon the throne to rule over the people (Mathew 1:1 NKJV). This testifies absolutely of the true Deity of Jesus Christ that He is the overall God of the universe.

11.9 Textual considerations of the Deity of Christ in the Bible

Furthermore, judging from the textual context and overall tone of the Scriptures, it is more than probable that the phrase in Romans, "who is over all God blessed forever" (Romans 9:5 NKJV) refers to Jesus the Messiah. As explained, Christ is the supreme God, which is in agreement, not only within Paul's own writings, but also with the other biblical authors. Whereas Paul refers to Christ as *"over all God"* (Romans 9:5 NKJV); John refers to Him as the *one and only God* and the *true God* (John 1:18; 1 John 5:20 NKJV). In Hebrews He is referred to as *the God* and unchangeable Creator, and *YHWH* (Heb. 1: 8 -12 NKJV). Peter refers to Him as *"the God and Savior"* (2 Pet. 1:1 NKJV); and Jude refers to Him as *"the only Master and Lord"* (Jude 1:4 NKJV). Timothy mentions Him as "For there is one God and one mediator between God and men, the man Christ Jesus" (1 Tim 2:5 NKJV). These are people who saw Him, ate with Him and lived with Him and their testimonies are true and cannot withstand the test of time. Paul claims that all things are from God and through Christ. Paul wrote: 'from Him and through Him and to Him are all things" (Romans 11:36 NKJV). God alone is the source, the means, and the end of all things. It is therefore our duty to glorify God and worship Him forever and ever. Here the statement simply refers to God, whereas in some other statements, Paul has divided it between God and Christ, applying to God two of the prepositions that describe God's relationship as Creator to all things (*'from'* and *'for'* or *'to'*) and the third of these prepositions (*through*) to Christ (1 Corinthians 8:6 NKJV). Although Paul's formula does not appear precisely in this form elsewhere, there are several Jewish examples that Paul quotes from (Romans 11:36 NKJV). We realize that God is not only the agent or efficient cause of creation (*from him are all things*) and the final cause or goal of all things (*to him are all things*), but also the instrumental cause (*through whom are all things*). This expresses very well the typical Jewish monotheistic concern that God used no one else to carry out his work of creation, but accomplished it alone, solely by means of his own Word and/or His own Wisdom. Paul includes Christ in this exclusively divine work of creation by giving to him the role of instrumental cause; that is, He and He alone is due that great honor (1 Corinthians 8:6 NKJV). Paul's statements, when properly understood and interpreted in light of their immediate and overall biblical contexts, do not exclude Jesus from being God in the same sense that the Father is. On rare occasions, he also applies the title Lord to the Holy Spirit (e.g. 2 Cor. 3:17). Paul was simply applying two different divine titles, *God and Lord*, to both the Father and the Son in order to show that both Persons (together with the Holy Spirit) constitute the Holy Trinity, the one true God, Yahweh Almighty. As the anointed one of God, Jesus becomes the sovereign Lord that directs the course of history toward its full completion. He is the One to establish The Kingdom of God on earth in the future and judge all nations and kingdoms on earth, which will take place at His coming. This revelation changed Paul's life forever. For since his conversation on the road to Damascus, Paul personally encountered "*the great God and Savior Jesus Christ*" (Titus 2:13 NKJV). He knew the Christ he preached was from the line of David *according to the flesh* and as to His divine nature, He is *over all God blessed forever*. It was not only Paul or the Apostles that knew much about the true nature of Jesus. For down through the centuries people have been discovering the same truth about Jesus Christ: that He was entirely different from any other person in history. You may begin by following Him as only a man, but if you stay with Him long enough you will finally know Him. Someday, like doubting Thomas, with all doubts gone, you will fall at His feet by saying, "*My Lord and my God*" (John 20:28 NKJV).

11.10 Other considerations on the Deity of Christ

The Quran teaches that Jesus, the Word of God is God. If therefore Muslim say, *"We cannot accept the divinity of Jesus Christ because it doesn't make sense for God to have a Son,"* it only shows that they are making reason their final step rather than revelation. In addition, they are making what they think look more important than what God's revelation discloses. Jesus Christ said to the Jews, "I am giving you evidence that I am the One, "Your father Abraham rejoiced to see my day, and saw it and rejoiced" (John 8:56-59 NKJV). Muslims may mix up what Jesus claimed He was and what He said He was not. Even though Jesus Christ is God, He did not claim to be the same person as God (i.e. the Father). However, He claimed to have the same nature as God. That is, He claimed to be one with God in nature, in substance and in essence. He also claimed to have the same nature with God in being, in power and in glory. This is seen in the word *"one"* (John 10:30-33 NKJV). When Jesus said to the Jews *"I and my Father are one"* the word *"one"* used is not masculine, but neuter. It did not mean person, but thing. That means Jesus is of the same thing and of the same substance as God. The Bible says when Jesus claimed that He is God, the Jews took stones to kill Him not for anything else but for blasphemy, because they thought He a mere man, claims to be God (v.33).

The evidences put forward by the *True Revelation of Jesus Christ* concerning the deity of Jesus Christ is so profound and true and should be of great help to Muslims, Jews and the atheist. Furthermore, there can be no greater testimony of this claim than the radical change about in the life of Paul who was a former antichrist and hater of Christians. For a man, who spent a considerable amount of time and effort and persecuting the followers of Jesus, to suddenly convert and become one of them, shows how truthful and reliable his testimonies are. If Muslims were to deny any of the testimonies of the disciples of Jesus, it must not be that of Paul. There is no doubt therefore that Jesus Christ Himself chose Paul to bear witness of the truth concerning Him, so that those who have stabbed Him at the back with unbelief, will have nothing to dispute about when it comes to the true revelation of Jesus Christ. Just like many who today do not believe in Jesus Christ as God, the Jews failed to believe in Him despite the signs and wonders He did in their sight. Unfortunately, the Jews are still waiting for a Savior that had already come but was not accepted by the Jews.

In the book entitled *the Rabbi who found the Messiah*; Rabbi Yitzhak Kaduri, who had an encounter with the Messiah passed a note not to be opened until a year after his death. The little note he wrote showed that Jesus is the messiah the Jews have been waiting for. Even though the family of Rabbi Yitzhak is believed to have denied this, revival is said to be taken place among the students of Rabbi Yitzhak's and many of them are being saved by this revelation. Because of unbelief, Jesus called the Jews hypocrites when they opposed His healing on the Sabbath day. It is very difficult to convert people who are hypocrites. As for the Muslims, their major grounds for not accepting Jesus as the true Son of God is that God cannot have a son and that the Bible has been corrupted. An important question to consider is, "The Bible or the Quran, which one is older?" Where did Muslims get all the details about Jesus in the Quran from? If the Quran refers Muslims to the Christian Bible concerning the truth of this nature, that makes the Bible not corrupted. Where comes this doctrine that *"if you believe that Jesus is God, you are going to hell"*? (Quran 5:72). The Quran categorically states: *"They are unbelievers who say, 'God is the Messiah, Mary's son.' For the Messiah said, 'Children of Israel, serve God, my Lord and your Lord. Verily whoso associates with God anything, God shall prohibit him entrance to Paradise, and his refuge shall be the Fire; and wrongdoers shall have no helpers."* What does the Quran mean by unbelievers say, *"God is the Messiah"*? Who are the unbelievers? According to Muslims, unbelievers are Jews and Christians. They are the same people the Quran admonishes Muslims to consult if they are in doubt. If the children of Israel of whom the world owes monotheism and Christians who associate with the same true God are called unbelievers by Muslims, then what actually should Jews and Christians call Muslims? The Quran quotes the

Messiah as saying to the children of Israel that they will not go to heaven if they associate themselves with any other God. The children of Israel serve no other God apart from Yahweh, the true God of the universe (Exodus 20:2-6; Deut. 4:35 NKJV).

To lay more emphasis on the deity of Jesus Christ, the Bible simply exposes those who deny His Lordship. The Bible categorically states: "Who is the liar? It is whoever denies that Jesus is the Christ. Such a person is the antichrist, denying the Father and the Son" (1 John 2:22 NKJV). Moreover, serious consideration ought to be given to what the Bible says with regard to salvation: "Whoever believes in Jesus is not condemned, but whoever does not believe stands condemned already because they have not believed in the name of God's one and only Son" (John 3:18 NKJV). Why did the writer of the Quran say all the beautiful things about the miraculous birth of Jesus Christ and all the wonderful things He did, but denies His divinity? That may be termed as apostasy. There is certainly something wrong for refusing to encourage individuals to find for themselves whether the Bible is truly forged or whether it is authentic? It is equally wrong for some Muslims to play God by killing or ostracizing Moslems who choose to become Christians just because they took Jesus as their God. Since Muslims believe it is Jesus Christ who will come to judge the world, and Jesus has stated emphatically in the Bible through the Holy Spirit that those who do not believe in Him as the Son of God are already condemned (John 3:18 NKJV), is it not obvious that unbelievers and others who deny the Deity of Jesus Christ are condemned? Yes, the Scripture says they are already condemned. This is because such a person is separated from Christ and is a foreigner to the promise of God that comes through Jesus Christ. The greatest sin of condemnation according to the Scriptures is to neglect and reject Jesus Christ as the Son and Savior of the world. Since Jesus Christ is the only great remedy for the sins of man, rejecting and refusing to accept Him as Savior is the same as being condemned. This in short means each person on earth has himself or herself to blame if they do not accept Jesus as Lord and Savior.

There are many people who have shut themselves in darkness concerning the truth about Jesus Christ and that is because they have chosen to deny the Lordship of Jesus over their lives. Furthermore, when the deeds of the Imams and the Muslim traditional leaders are looked into properly, there is no doubt that just like the Sadducees and the Pharisees in the time of Jesus, they are looking for nothing better than their own self-interest. It will be more enlightening for them to remove the scales from their eyes, find the truth about Jesus and discard the ideologies and correct prejudices and presuppositions that have no substance regarding the Son of God. If the Quran and the Bible affirm that Jesus is *The Word of God*, then Jesus is truly God and also the Son of God and believing in Him as Lord and Savior will bring salvation, peace and harmony to Muslims and the rest of the world and not the least Jewish people.

Afterword

To end the volume one of this book about Jesus Christ is the greatest thing to take into consideration. This is because many will come from the four corners of the earth and will take their places at the feast with all believers of Jesus Christ in the kingdom of heaven (Mathew 8:11). A book of this sort is therefore to invite you to be a partaker of such a feast. All that you need is to put on the garment of Christ which is yours by heritage. You don't need to worry about how many sins you have committed in the past, because once you accept the Son of God, your sins will be something of the past. You may be worried about all the fun you are enjoying in life and thinking that Jesus came to take away all the joy from your life and replace them with rules that are impossible to live by. It is rather easier to have Jesus in your life than live your own life. Knowing Jesus is not about religion, but about a person who is ready to go beyond religious rites to completely embrace you no matter how sinful you are or have been. Jesus introduced to you in this book is the person that matters to your destiny. This is because He alone is able to save and give life. There is one thing that is unique about Jesus; He is the only one that is able to unlock the mystery of eternal life and shuts the doors of hell against you. He puts Himself in your place by exchanging your death with the life that He alone is able to give. Many people including Muslim, Jews and atheists have encountered Jesus and are transformed in the hearts with new hope in a Savior who can offer love that no one else can offer. There are also many that have been set free from drugs, alcohol, fornication, adultery and now even murderers, wicked men and women who surrendered their lives to Him were given new hope and new life. People that have gone through depression for many years have testified how Jesus delivered them. In our generation today, people who are curious to know about Jesus have always been satisfied and content about the amazing glory and the power of love that surrounds Jesus. The most thrilling thing about Jesus is the forgiveness message, that we are to forgive our enemies and love them, clothe them and otherwise meet their needs. No other person in the history of the world ever taught such a great message of love. This is the reason for the rise of humanitarian societies and philanthropists in the world, taking a classical example from the demonstration of Jesus love.

Whilst it might be deception to follow other religious leaders, there is one thing about Jesus that differs. He is greater than the great figures of men in history. He is greater than Mohammed, Krishna, Buddha, Julius Caesar, Abraham Lincoln or Napoleon Bonaparte or any religious leader of our time. Just ponder over this for a while, that there is none that can be compared to Jesus. Surrounding your life completely over to such a trustworthy person gives greater security than any unbeliever can imagine. The Prophet Mohammed himself testified that he was a sinner and that Jesus was born without sin. This makes Jesus the greatest and the most righteous person that ever walked on the face of our earth. It is He alone that answers the questions of life: *Who am I? Why am I here?* And *where am I going?* Before you write Him off, remember the claims He makes about life and the reason why we are here on earth. All the great men of history and the religious men and prophets of old are all dead and no one can guarantee where they are now. Jesus however guarantees and assures those who follow Him of eternal life whilst none of those in history ever did so. Even those who in our lifetime posed as false Christs died miserably without saving themselves. No great religious leaders could guarantee whether they would be saved or not. The Bible affirmatively states that Jesus is the Way, the Truth and the Life and anyone who wants to make heaven can ONLY do so through Him. Jesus is still alive today and the Quran confirms it! Jesus is still speaking to the world through the Christian Bible and by the power of His Holy Spirit invites everyone to forsake their sin, take up their cross and follow Him (Matthew 16:24). To take the cross to follow Him entails self-denial and sacrifice. You can easily do it, for that is the best choice to make for your life.

Making a Covenant of Salvation with
Jesus Christ as Lord and Savior

Jesus died and shed His blood for your sake so that after this life you will have an everlasting life with God in heaven (John 14:2 NKJV). Jesus has assured us that He is the resurrection and the life, and you cannot bypass Him to heaven. Are you saved? If not, then read Romans 10:9-10 and invite Jesus into your life. Jesus calls us to repent. Ask God to forgive you the sins you sinned against Him and many others and you will have the power to forgive others of the sins they have also sinned against you.

If you have not yet accepted Jesus Christ, you may do so here by saying with me: Father, I come to you in the name of Jesus. I am a sinner and need salvation. I ask you to forgive me all my sins and cleanse me from all my sins. I renounce Satan and all his ways and believe that Jesus Christ is the Son of God. I accept Jesus Christ as my Lord and Savior. Grant me your Holy Spirit and write my name in the book of life. Thank you, Father in the mighty name of Jesus, Amen!

Find the opportunity to look for a Bible believing church to attend and share this with others, especially your own families. Finally let me end by saying that together we are one, because we have the same hope in God through Jesus Christ, the Son of God. We thank God for revealing to us the hidden things concerning what is to come by the power of His Holy Spirit. To God be all glory and praise and honor in Jesus Christ. Choose wisely and prayerfully. I also hope you will have the opportunity to read Volume 2 of this book.

God bless you and keep you in perfect peace. Amen!

References

Foxe's Book of Martyrs, Christian Classic by John Foxe

The Rabbi who Found the Messiah: *The story of Yitzhak Kaduri and his prophecies at the end time* by Carl Gallups

(Mahmoud M. Ayoub, The Quran and Its Interpreters: The House of *Imran* [State University of New York Press (SUNY), 1992], Volume II, p. 94).

F. W. Nietzsche, *The AntiChrist*, trans. By H. L. Mencken ('Torrance, CA: The Noontide Press, 1980)

Sais I-Nursi, *The Rays*, The Fifth Ray, p. 493, as quoted in Harun Yahya, *Jesus will Return*, (London, Ta Ha, 2001), p. 66

Murray J. Harris, Jesus as God

(The International Standard Bible Encyclopedia, James Orr, Howard –Severance, 1930).

The encyclopedia of Christianity, Volume 4 by Erwin Fahlbusch, 2005

ISBN 978-0-8028-2416-5 pages 52-56

The Epistle of Barnabas from the Early Church Fathers – Volume 1

The *Annals* by Tacitus; written 109 A.C.E.; translated by Alfred John Church and William Jackson Brodribb

Watt, *Muhammad at Medina*, Oxford UP, 1956, p. 196.

Schäefer, Peter, *Jesus in the Talmud*, Princeton University Press, 2007

Grant, Michael, Jesus: An Historian's Review of the Gospels, Scribner, 1995

Tacitus' Annals by Ronald Mellor 2010 Oxford University Press

Jewish Antiquities, Books XVIII-XIX (Loeb Classical Library, 433)

L. H. Feldman

The Concise Encyclopedia of Islam, Harper & Row, 1989, p. 64

The Holy Bible, English Standard Version

Gandhi, M.K. (1955), *My Religion*, Compiled/edited by Bharatan Kumarappa

George, S. K. (1947): Gandhi's Challenge to Christianity

Duin, Julia (2001), *Christians face dismal plight in Islamic nations*, Washington Times, November 6.

Hamilton, Victor (1990), *Genesis 1-17* (Grand Rapids: Eerdmans).

The Teachings of Imam Muhammed al-Bàqùr by Arzina R. Lalani

Bibles: King James version

New International Version

New Living Translation

New English Standard Version

History of the Christian Church *Philip Schaff 23*

https://www.youtube.com/watch?v=RVvsmc5YsGg or at https://www.youtube.com/watch?v=WjUXd4qW9mg.

C.S. Lewis, *Mere Christianity* (Sn Francisco: Harper, 2001)

http://y-jesus.com/more/jcg-jesus-claim-god/

Lewis, Ibid

Philip Schaff, *The Person of Christ*: The Miracle of History (1913)

Printed in the United States
By Bookmasters